Archetype to Zest

26 Essays for the Curious

Ethel Erickson Radmer

Archetype to Zest: 26 Essays for the Curious
Copyright © 2015 Ethel Erickson Radmer
All rights reserved

ISBN 978-0-9651182-4-8   0-9651182-4-X

Printed in the United States of America
Published by Euphonia Publishing, North Carolina

Cover photo of author by Bonnie Scott

Titles also by Ethel Erickson Radmer

Knowing Sarah: Lost Arts, Health Practices and Moral Guideposts

Walking the Rails: My Childhood in Whitehall

My Odyssey with Two Uncommon Boys: A Trip to the Western States

Conversations with Carl: My Journey through Grief

The Cheshire Cat Syndrome: My Adventures with Arthritis

CONTENTS

ARCHETYPE

November 2013

Have you noticed the plethora of books recently with the word *Archetype* in their title or in their subject matter? I have. And without making a long list and losing your attention right off the bat, just know that authors in the fields of philosophy, psychology, alternative medicine and especially personal growth are BIG on this word! Myss, Chopra, Houston, Boulter and Bolen among others—oops, enough, I'll stop the listing—are some of the writers who attach strong meaning to it and almost simultaneously and collectively elevate the attention of millions of readers to the word. I've read a bunch of these books and, though my brain is working, I either don't agree or am still not sure what they are talking about or driving at. But that didn't stop me, a year ago, from going ahead and giving a talk about the subject to a small group of metaphysical enthusiasts.

Archetype is not a light and frivolous word or fun, at least to me, because I am skeptical of all the extrapolations that authors make from it and the limitations they impose, particularly on a person—I don't want to be stuck in a category. And in deciding about archetypes you have to think too hard. The word is so serious and clever and deep. It makes the authors and others who manage to fit it into their conversation sound so profound. How smart and clever that they have figured it out.

Is a cold ham sandwich an archetype? Maybe, maybe not. If you say "he's as romantic as a cold ham sandwich," it probably is.

Might any human being qualify? Yes, if they fit into premade slots like 'macho man,' 'hapless buffoon,' 'princess,' 'self-centered egotist' and 'star-crossed lover.' And if someone keeps adding labels to an endless collection of traits, then every human being on the planet can be included in at least one and probably many more archetypes, if we think hard enough. So you are an archetype of something or an archetype is you.

Can a belief, such as I had as a young university student—that psychologists are more normal than psychiatrists (my field was occupational therapy and I mixed with both professionals), meet the synonym-filled definition of archetype? Maybe if it is called 'the unsubstantiated idea' or 'the prejudiced thinker' or another collection of basic traits of a thing.

So, there are endless categories for an archetype—enough for every person, for any idea with substance (although if an idea has little or no substance that category might garner an archetypal label of 'ideas with no substance.' Archetypes are pervasive, found not only in real people but in story lines in real life and in fiction and more.

Places you see and hear of archetypes most frequently are in Jungian psychology where you might say the love affair with the word began; they are present in literature—books and plays— where the archetypical workings have been honed to a fine art; and if you open your eyes (I'm speaking for my 'pop culture specific' woefully ignorant self), archetypes are rampant in popular culture— entertainment with movies, television and video games. Art can be archetypal and one can find archetypes in art. Images in art, such as paintings and sculptures, even in the abstract, can activate archetypes in the viewers' mind and evoke an emotional response.

And heck, you can find archetypes in the Bible if you look and give it enough thought. Make them up. See the parable of the loaves and fishes showing us an archetypal belief that if we believe, we can make plenty out of nothing. The authors of the books of the Bible didn't know the word archetype nor probably imagine the concept, at least to write about, but we literary types and story tellers can spot them.

And the ancient Greeks in Greek mythology—where the use of the word archetype seems to have begun—had them too. Zeus was the god king tyrant. Persephone was the young maiden, rebellious daughter and most remembered as the perpetual damsel in distress, the woman who has yet to come into her own. Hera was the faithful wife but scorned.

Philosophers, with Plato the Greek as a foundation, talk about forms that embody the basic characteristics of a thing. That describes an archetype.

In a world apart from the above examples is a field of classification that we sometimes have reason to intersect—mathematics—that has its own use and meaning of the word 'archetype.' It is an esoteric landscape. In mathematics, the phrase *canonical example* is frequently used to mean 'archetype, standard example.' In geometry you find *canonical forms, canonical vector field, canonical polyhedron* and *canonical coordinates*, all archetypes.

Spelling it out further, Carl Jung, a Swiss psychiatrist and psychotherapist (1875 - 1961), who founded analytical psychology, was the first to develop a school of psychological thinking that revolved around archetypes, where they were the theme, the core that everything is wrapped around. Archetypes encompassed groupings of all the stuff in the unconscious, in memories, visions and dreams. Religion, fairy tales and mythology were part of the mix, with actions and characters in them loaded with symbols and motifs. Jung saw these as conscious representations and called them archetypes. He figured out what the archetype was and made interpretations of behavior based on the archetype. He was a theorist, a teacher and he had a private practice. His intention with a patient was to help them uncover their unconscious and to make it conscious. Then, with the help of archetypes, they work to better understand the patient's behavior and hopefully relieve pain and discomfort. Some of the archetypes that Jung came up with are the *mother archetype, the shadow, the persona, the anima* (female aspect in the collective unconscious), *the animus* (male aspect in the collective unconscious), *father, family, child, maiden, hero, wise old man, trickster* (clown or magician who makes trouble) and most important of all the archetypes that Jung worked with—*the self.* To realize the self is our goal in life, he would say.

Literature abounds with archetypes. It seems to be up to the literary intelligentsia to give meaning and set rules distinguishing lines of difference in archetypes and other related words, such as synonyms. Fiction authors use archetypes in their character development and in planning the plot or story line of a book or play or film.

In the personal growth realm, Jean Houston, in person in Carlsbad in 2012, spoke to a group of us about archetypes, along with Deepak Chopra. As a well-known author, actor, performer and innovative thinker, Jean put it all together on stage. She brilliantly play acted different characters, revealing the why and what of their behavior. It was meant to provoke our own thinking about the archetypes that we all have a turn at playing in our real lives. Deepak said that spiritual solutions to our problems arise when our awareness is expanded. Your archetype can awaken powers within you and help you become fulfilled. They are the keys to your true and amazing destiny. So, I sum up, archetypes expand our awareness of ourselves.

Caroline Myss, a medical intuitive and a mystic, who writes books and has a website about archetypes, says we are intimately bound to archetypes and that not one aspect of our life is without an archetypal thread—not one. She sees that archetypes help us reach our highest potential.

Bolen, a Jungian analyst, speaks of our inner archetypes, using the power of myth in our lives and Boulter writes of the feminine consciousness and archetypes. Douglas Soccio, a Professor of Philosophy, writes about archetypes of wisdom in philosophy.

That is a little sample of what the loudest voices in the personal growth movement, psychology and philosophy are saying about this word. Let's be playful—there are no 'wrong' ideas—with this discussion. In the interest of fun, let's put Chopra, Houston, Myss, Bolen, Boulter and Soccio together in my made-up categories of 'brainy seekers of meaning,' or 'behavioral-study enthusiasts' or 'creative thinkers.' So now I enlist you! *You* have creative thoughts. You can make up your own archetypal groupings.

All this while we've been learning about the A word by usage and in context. It would have been logical for me to define the word right away at the beginning of this essay. But, I like to lead by example! And you can find a lot more examples throughout your day than the ones I've given you so far. I'm overdue, yes I know; it's time to come up with the roots of the word and a solid definition that inevitably has to use other words that are close to it in meaning. I don't want us to have pre-formed conclusions, decided in advance, in this case the predetermined definition of the word archetype. And I think that the meaning of a word has the potential of being in flux if people's common usage of the word calls for that.

The actual word *archetype* can be traced back to ancient Greece (8th to 6th centuries BC to the end of antiquity - 600 AD). *Arkhetupos* (original) and *tupos* (pattern. model or type) are the root words and the combined meaning is "an 'original pattern' of which all similar people, things or ideas are derived and copied." Archetype in Greek was translated into the Latin word *archetypum*. And then the word *archetype* took hold in the sixteenth century in England with Sir Francis Bacon's (1561 – 1626) intellectually innovative, prolific and influential writings and Shakespeare's (1564 - 1616) plays. Shakespeare's plays are full of character archetypes, the types that appear over and over again in literature, film and theater—'The Fool' as Falstaff in *King Lear* for one. Amidst much controversy, many people have theorized that Bacon is the real author behind Shakespeare's work.

A word of warning: the word archetype is not to be confused with the words stereotype, cliché, synonym or metaphor, even though those words might be used to define the word archetype. The literary intelligentsia would be after you for that slip-up and there are plenty of people who do interchange those words.

The difference between archetype and *stereotype* is this. Stereotypes are predictable, clichéd and oversimplified qualities given to a person or thing. Archetypes are more complex. Stereotypes are generally thought to be bad, but archetypes are good. We elevate 'archetype' above the fray of less well thought of nouns.

A *cliché* differs just a little from an archetype in that cliché is old and tired, imitative and copycat. Archetype is fresh.

A *synonym* is a word that has the same or nearly the same meaning as another word in a language. And there are a lot of synonyms that describe archetype. Here are a few: antecedent, ancestor, forerunner, precursor, predecessor, prototype, form, ideal, model, original, paradigm, pattern, standard, classic, exemplar, perfect specimen, embodiment and quintessence.

A *metaphor*, again according to my American Heritage dictionary, is a 'figure of speech in which a word or phrase that ordinarily designates one thing is used to designate another, thus making an implicit comparison as *in the evening of life.*' I get that, but can *evening of life* also be a category for an archetype—as in 'all of the things experienced in the late years'?

My head gets dizzy with studying the differences and finding examples. I don't think I am able to repeat what I said, even if I wanted. And please don't ask me to figure it out again. But *you* are most welcome to make archetypes your own!

Like our new friend, the archetypal *trickster* in myths and traditions everywhere, play tricks, be a mischievous and foolish knave, cross boundaries. Blur distinctions and be funny. Being laughed at and admired with awe at the same time goes with the territory. You operate within a hallowed context of the literacracy and simultaneously *you* are sacred. We all need the laughter and mischief of the trickster archetype, beyond what is safe for us and what we are willing to do, in order to satisfy our own repressed impulses and thus survive and flourish in this crazy world. Oh you trickster!

Ethel Erickson Radmer

BEE and BUTTERFLY

November 2013

My dad, Arvid B Erickson, had many hives of bees in the 1940s and 50s, pollinating fields and making honey, throughout the coulees of Wisconsin that surrounded our small town of Whitehall. That is where my love affair with the honey bee began.

The marvels of the bee are astonishing. Multiply one bee by thousands and we see a community of these winged insects that is highly organized and efficient, almost beyond belief. Let's take Apis mellifera, the scientific species name for the honeybee, as my devoted focus of attention. Know that there are 25,000 species of bee flying out there all over the world including the well-known bumble bees, carpenter bees and stingless bees. But I'll stick with the honey bee.

It's not a surprise by now for you to realize that the honeybee is my favorite tiny, winged creature, along with the butterfly and, like a lot of other honeybee lovers, I have good reasons for it. I want the bees to bask in all the attention I'm giving them. They deserve it especially now in tough times and even with all the notice they and their honey have garnered since almost the beginning of humanity. Well, we're uncertain of Bible dates, but a swarm of bees, wild honey and honeycomb are all mentioned in Bible verses, as far as you can go to the Old Testament books of Genesis, Exodus and

Leviticus, the first three books in the Bible, as well as other books in the Old and New Testaments. And bees and people gathering honey are seen in Egyptian art back to 15,000 years ago. Those were the wild ones. Honey bees spread north to Europe and somewhere along the way were domesticated.

First off to know is the cast of characters in the caste of bees called a colony and the honey bee's living quarters. Their hive home is a square, usually 18" x 18" for brood space, covered, wooden box or boxes stacked to arm height for the beekeeper to be able to reach inside. Eleven wooden frames that each hang and hold a wax honeycomb fill the boxes. The comb started with a thin foundation sheet put in by the beekeeper that the worker bees build on to make honeycomb cells. The hexagonal honeycomb is an architectural and engineering wonder. The hexagon design, as opposed to squares or triangles, makes it stronger and more compact, contributes to a more efficient use of labor and quantity of wax and it maximizes storage area for the honey. We don't know if it is the bee's incredible oval, small sesame seed-size brain and the bee's natural skills or is it physical forces that make the wax that the worker bee drops in place on the sheet and keeps warm with its body, naturally form into a multi-hexagonal grid. Perhaps it is both. The bee's comb is near-perfect in its geometry and beautiful to see. But how did the bees learn to do that? Well, with hundreds of thousands of neurons in a honeybee brain they can learn, memorize long routes to sites and back, recall a multitude of tasks quickly and teach other bees by communicating with a figure-8 'waggle dance.'

There are three castes in a colony or swarm or community of honeybees. The queen bee, the worker bee and the drone are differentiated by their tasks in life and by variations in their appearance.

The queen bee, as long as she is not too tattered and torn by prey or the elements, lasts about three to five years, much longer than her drones and worker bees. She is always fertile and is the most important bee in the colony, for she is the mother of almost all the bees in the hive. The workers cater to her lavishly when she is chosen as a bee larva to become queen. She is fed royal jelly by the workers for a couple of weeks until she matures into the queen. The royal jelly is made of chewed-up pollen mixed with a chemical from the nursing worker bee's head. That mush of pollen is what makes her a queen. With that diet she becomes one and one-half times the size of the other bees and fertile. Then she mates with a series of drones, one time with each because the drone dies with the trauma. Strong drones—to pass on those genes—fly outside and far away from the hive to meet and mate with and give the queen their sperm. Then she comes back to lay up to 1500 eggs or more per day. The fertilized eggs become worker bees and the unfertilized eggs become drones. Another job of the queen is to produce and disseminate pheromones that suppress the development of ovaries in all the female worker bees in the hive and prevent them from laying eggs. In studies, royal jelly has been fed to roosters, pigs, chickens and fruit flies by curious scientists and the life span of the roosters and pigs increased by about a third. The flies grew bigger and more fertile and the chickens either started laying again or laid twice as many eggs. Outgrowing and outliving seems to be the result. Is Royal jelly the panacea for infertility? I've eaten it for general good health and so have thousands of others. I don't think it can harm.

All drones, up to only 3000 in the hive, are male. They do not have stingers so are powerless to protect themselves. They have no chores but to mate with the queen and only once. With a barbed sex organ the drone dies after mating. Their life span is about three months. Whatever drones are still alive in the fall are no longer of any use for stand-by breeding and are expelled from the hive. Poor drones. They live without purpose until the one peak sexual act to pass on sperm and thus propagate the hive and death follows.

The worker bees do everything that needs doing and die young—6 weeks in the summer with a heavy work load—and if they are young in the fall they could last the winter. These daughters of the queen far outnumber the drones—30,000 or more per hive. They make honey and royal jelly, produce wax, feed the larvae, nurse, clean, build, guard and they collect pollen and nectar from flowering plants, thus pollinating plants over nearly one-third of the food crops in the world, one of the most vital and under-appreciated jobs in agriculture and witness how badly we've treated honeybees in their possible demise. None of the worker bees are sexually mature, except for the one selected to be queen. She becomes fertile with the royal jelly fed to her as a larva. With a barbed stinger that tears out their abdomen, workers can only sting once and they die. As the drones, using their barbed sex organ, die after one mating.

All the honeybees, including the queen, workers and drones, have some outstanding features and traits in common. Their eyes have to be seen to be believed. To see in poor light a bee uses three simple eyes, called ocelli, positioned on the top of its head. In addition, each bee has two compound eyes wrapping partway around the head, a marvel to behold and a puzzle for us to figure out. What do the bees see? The drone has the biggest wrap-around eyes and so is easy to spot. Each compound eye has many hundreds of single eyes positioned next to each other (somewhat like our retina), each having its own lens and each looking in a different direction. The bee's brain puts them all together and sees an overall image and it is big. They have a nearly 180 degree field of vision and an almost infinite field, near and far, albeit at a low resolution. Bee's eyes are very good at seeing polarized light (good for cloudy days) and detecting colors—especially yellow-green, blue and ultraviolet light, but not so much red—and are better than us for spotting motion. The bee goes for the flower blowing in the wind.

The honey bee has another sensing organ: two antennae in the front of its head with thousands of tiny sensors that detect smell. That information helps the bees to identify flowers, bees in their colony, water and people like us.

Bees are known for their organization and cooperation. They live in an amazing community and pull off remarkable feats to take care of themselves that has been admired and even emulated for centuries. We are still learning from them, such as in studies by cognitive researchers M. Lehmann, D. Gustav and C. G. Galizia revealing that honey bees do their best learning in the morning or in 'uncertainty monitoring' researchers, C. J. Perry and A. B. Barron, finding out that when faced with a decision that the bees are likely to get wrong, the bees opt out. Thinking about thinking, which the 'opting out' could be, requires self-awareness and it would be a remarkable thing if it found that a bee does indeed have reflection and an awareness of itself.

Bees swarm or gather en mass and in motion to leave the hive and set up residence somewhere else when a new queen takes over a colony or when they have no more room and they have to move on. They could disappear in a swarm with the queen and not be seen again, with the beekeeper left bereft. Or the mysterious 'colony collapse disorder' might be blamed when all the bees leave the hive in a swarm, abandoning the queen.

As beautiful and smart as a honey bee is and as noble and industrious as their communal work demonstrates in so brief a time on earth they are having a tough time now, trying to accommodate to changes in their world that intersect ours.

It's a harsh world for the bees. It has been especially rough the last couple of decades. Something is killing them off and hives are disappearing. Scientists have no definitive answers but there are some likely suspects—pollution and toxins, mites, viruses, disease and cities taking over farm land making for less foraging territory. My own speculation is that we have thrown off the bee's ecosystem with unnatural interventions, such as antibiotics and honey water to stretch the hives survival. Their balance is thrown to the winds. For any honeybee lover it is disheartening to see their dwindling numbers, probably a result of what we as humans are doing to our planet. Pesticides that farmers use on their crops can scramble the honey bee's brain circuitry according to some research. And all the while the honey bee is doing good things for us by pollinating the flowers on the planet. It isn't fair!

But we can appreciate the honeybees that we still have and the honey, royal jelly, beeswax and propolis, made by the worker bees and the pollen they collect and bring back to the hive. All are taken from the hive by we humans (sorry bees! is this sting attack time?) and are used by us as food and health supplements and aids and yes, even bee venom for disease.

It was the worker bees who stung me for health. In the summer of 1977 in Vermont, as a grown-up, I got stung intentionally 390 times by the same wonderful creatures that provided us with honey throughout my growing-up years.

Why ever would I do that? 'Bee venom therapy' was being done by one beekeeper and guru of stings, Charles Mraz (died in 1999 at age 94), to many people with arthritis and I was having joint pain and swellings. The honey bees gave up their lives for me and I felt a little bad. I don't know if it was the bees or other things that helped, but I have been fine for three decades since. I thank the bees for whatever they might have done for me. And I didn't mind the stings at all.

They are glorious creatures with a sturdy looking exoskeleton surrounding the thorax and abdomen that is donned in strong colors and stripes of golden orange and onyx black that may ward off potential predators. Their weapon is a stinger and the female workers will pour out of their hive to attack, though they are not aggressive unless provoked.

As a honey bee might see a polarized light beam (light waves vibrating in one direction rather than many directions that can cause glare) by reflection and thus be able to navigate on cloudy days, I reflect on the past filled with my love of the honey bee. I've watched it in flight, drawing nectar, filling the bee hive boxes, swarming and stinging. That's what bees do. I've learned from them. And I think about their future. I want the best for them and maybe nature will find a way to make their lives better and longer. Or maybe we will come to our senses and make the world a healthier place for the Queen and her children. They are an inspiration with their tenacity to carry on. Their good traits are to emulate and ponder. And, like the bees, I think my best thoughts in the morning.

Emily Dickenson wrote several poems about bees and I honor the bees in my life and their death with two stanzas from Nature LXV:

> His feet are shod with gauze,
> His helmet is of gold;
> His breast, a single onyx
> With chrysoprase, inlaid.
> His labor is a chant,
> His idleness a tune;
> Oh, for a bee's experience
> Of clovers and of noon!

But the butterfly! The cocoon transformed to soar! Another glorious insect. Known for its beauty and not as much its pedigree. It is this other small winged insect of my two loved fliers. *The bee is not afraid of me, I know the butterfly.* Emily Dickenson brought them together in Nature LVIII. We had a mutual lack of fear, the bee and I, in our intimate stinging days. And yes, Emily and I know the butterfly.

> Two butterflies went out at noon
> And waltzed above a stream,
> Then stepped straight through the firmament
> And rested on a beam; Nature XVIII

This is not a thorough background check but just to remind us from those long ago science classes that the life cycles of the honey bee and of the butterfly are nearly the same. Both start out as an egg, change into a larva or caterpillar, transform to the pupa or chrysalis stage and then burst forth into a flying bee or a soaring butterfly. As an *imago* or adult the honey bee and butterfly share similar body parts—thorax, abdomen, antennae, hearing organs positioned by the antennae for bees and under the wings on the butterfly and both have two compound eyes plus three simple eyes for the bee. Four wings attach to the thorax of both the bee and butterfly. The bees' average wingspan is one inch, way smaller than most butterflies, and honey bees fly faster at 15 mph than the butterfly at 12 mph. They both feed on nectar and pollen, plus honey for the bees and thus they pollinate the planet. But here a big difference begins. The aesthetics trump all other attributes and accomplishments. It is in the beauty of the butterfly wings!

For beauty and brevity's sake—there are 17,500 species of butterflies worldwide and 750 in the U.S.A.—let's take just the Monarch butterfly, a favorite of mine and of much of the population to admire and then, as a footnote, take one more species for variety and for the romance of their flying in my birth home state of Wisconsin, the Spring Azure butterfly.

The Monarch, named after royalty, goes by the scientific name of *Danaus lexippus*. Its colors are of royalty, too. The bright, contrasting colors of orange, black and white cover the gossamer wings, looking like leaded, stained glass. The veins and margins of black stripes are the 'lead' to set off and hold together the orange, varied oval and rectangular shapes throughout the scaled surface of the wing. Multiple white eye spots dot the edges. This stunning pattern on the wings has been programed, through decades of evolution, in the genes. It's a knockout, an attention grabber for the predator to be attracted to but also to be warned. The Monarch is poisonous to predators like frogs, birds, mice and lizards (but not to humans), because of the poisonous (to the predators) milkweed that the butterfly consumes in its larval stage. Their beauty is a double-edged sword. A Monarch's wings, fluttering at a rate of five to twelve times a second (slower than most other butterflies), are part of its fascination. Those wings take several generations of butterflies on a migration every year from the cold north to the warm south. Their survival is threatened in similar ways to the bee—pollution, toxins, the danger of human encroachment, as the bees have lost their fields to roam and, for the Monarch, losing the land of milkweed that is vital to the larvae. But I'm optimistic that something will change to the good.

Of the thousands of butterflies sparkling the skies around our globe, showing off an incredible display of patterns and design, using various shapes and stripes and spots, and an array of colors beyond our artist's palette, I have a special fondness for the Spring Azure butterfly, with its own beauty in coloration and design. It is small, some the size of a fingernail, as many butterflies are—do we even notice them? Look carefully at this tiny, delicate jewel, which azure is—a blue mineral used as a gem, the color of the sky on a clear summer's day. White dots scatter across the velvet surface of the wing with scalloped edges. And *Celastrina Iadon* is its scientific name. You exist in the annals of science and I hope you last forever.

How ever was she and all the other 17,500 species of butterflies created in this fickle world of chance and elimination? Its' metamorphosis I think is a metaphor for all of creation. It seems a miracle to see the butterflies mingle in the endless air. Beauteous insects, sharing that vast space above us with whomever is brave enough to fly.

Oh, to be free as a butterfly. Showing its striking beauty with swirls and flights of fancy. An unbound spirit. So in the moment. I'll admire you up close and afar to the end of my earthly days.

CONSCIOUSNESS

November 2013

Semantics are important. From a very young age on, the meaning of words was a bottom-line criterion for me of how I might proceed with my actions. Here's a word *consciousness* that I heard in adult discourse and I understood it to be our *awake state of awareness*. I absorbed the word into my lexicon like it was made for me and I've been fascinated with it ever since. I've watched its 'coming out' into general awareness through the years. It wasn't given any respect by research scientists a few decades ago (in my early professional life as an occupational therapist). It was too much in the realm of the unknowable, too nebulous in concept for someone to be solid about what it was and how it could be studied. My dad was a model for all this in his many arguments (yes we used the word argument straight-out, rather than discussion, since there was a big difference in views, but a very civil argument at the same time) with people and their beliefs, because of his parsing of the word and phrase that he and others used in their arguments. Consciousness was a word that seemed, in my mind, to fill the void of the puzzling and unknown, to account for the beyond and what was not explainable.

The concept of consciousness existed, I'm speculating, from the earliest human's articulations of words like mind and spirit. The origin of the actual word goes back at least to the early 1600s with the Latin word *conscius* meaning 'knowing' and 'aware.' Also in the 1600s, the philosopher, John Locke, defined the self through a 'continuity of consciousness' and the mathematician and philosopher, Rene Descartes, made his famous observation in 1637, "I think; therefore I am" in his writings about the mind–body duality. Even though philosophers had been aware of and written about consciousness for centuries, psychologists and eventually neuroscientists, lagging behind those long-ago groundbreakers, but at the same time at the forefront of the modern age, saw a need for the word, took hold of it, gave it careful notice, did research and started talking and writing about it.

We are aware! We know that we know! Like Descartes said, "I am" and also "Whatever I know, I know intuitively that I am." By definition of consciousness being an awareness of ourselves, we are conscious beings and have consciousness.

For all the fuss, consciousness is similar to and included in the meaning and definition of a lot of other words. You could almost use them interchangeably. Try these for size: sense, observation, capacity, soul, spirit, seat of thought, mind, reason, think, reflect, ruminate, notice, realize, percipient, knowledge, subliminal self, subconscious and ego. Well, their size is a little small for this big word consciousness and not inclusive enough, as I see it. What I imagine is a 'state of possession'—that is to have and hold a sense of an entity—of me and of you and other people and to own a sense of things and of action. Awareness of all of this is the core of being conscious.

What more is different is that consciousness is more inclusive of all our experience. It is a state of being aware of being. It is a condition of existence that knows it exists, of awareness of being aware, of knowing that we know. It's a state of perceiving, comprehending, experiencing, discovering, and being cognizant of our own cognition. The word consciousness is active, emits energy and is alive.

Where does consciousness reside? Is its locale physical? Or is it in a realm that we can't detect with our senses? Most scientists and behavioral professionals believe, say and write that the physical brain housed in the skull is home to our consciousness. All emotions and feelings—ideas, wants, memories and everything to do with thinking are in the mind which is in the brain. The brain is the control center for the body, receiving and sending messages to all parts of the body. These messages travel along nerves, which are like electrical wires, pulsing electricity.

Nine-tenths of the space in our brain, that is its total volume, is the cerebrum. It contains some white matter that links nerve cells with other parts of the brain, but most people's attention is given to the gray matter or cerebral cortex, above the white matter, where thoughts, ideas and decisions happen and where we become aware of what our senses tell us. My dad spoke of gray matter often. "Use your gray matter" or "use your noggin" (in more colloquial terms), to solve a problem or to think something through. I imagined those thoughts traveling at lightning speed. So the gray matter is at least one place where consciousness exists, according to students of the brain. But the mind, to use that term somewhat interchangeably with consciousness, is working in many parts of the brain in a very complex system. That means that our awareness of ourselves and others and objects, or our consciousness, is operating throughout the brain. Will we ever be able to figure it out? However do we measure awareness? Well, the scientific community believes it is physical but they don't have proof. They are confident that we will eventually know precisely where and how being conscious works; that the searching for connections of neurons will 'voila' produce consciousness.

But there is a world of skepticism about this line of thinking and I'm one of the skeptics. I see their explanation as so inadequate. The best the defenders can say is "I don't know." The concept of awareness of self and others does not seem to me to have physical properties. The physical is real, observable and measurable. And you can't see consciousness, even with the strongest microscope. It's conceivable that some microscopic enigma of an 'in and out' neutrino (no electrical charge) or electron could be found and ascribed to consciousness, but it is tough for me to imagine. Consciousness, in my conception, is limitless and formless. It is 'being.' It is not a physical thing.

Is there an infinite consciousness? The skeptics and dissenters of the 'contained in the brain' thinking expand awareness to the whole universe, though I remind that the universe is still finite. But the infinite self, some say, is in the whole. Our awareness merges with a universal energy. The same consciousness, that orchestrates the whole world and beyond dwells within each of us. That might be hard to imagine too, but, very significantly for me, it gives the broad view, the big picture, the overall concept which I want to see with anything of importance.

Do animals have consciousness? From the honey bee and sparrow to the elephant and dolphin, they seem to have some degree of self-awareness. Pet owners are on the front lines to see consciousness in their animals of all sorts and to tell stories such as dogs taking on the cancer of their masters (yes, I know two!). An African grey parrot named Alex, as studied by Irene Pepperberg, associated words with meanings and performed many cognitive tasks (signs of awareness) even at the level of human toddlers. And as a coup for research, Alex could talk! And, me talking about another sense—seeing, try connecting steadily with the eyes of a tiger in an open-air zoo (I did in India) or the eyes of a dolphin in the Pacific off Morea—I have done that also, my eyes up close to its eye and, with my arms under its belly, I felt a profound, deep connection with the dolphin. There was a bond that (dare I be presumptive?) we both established at the very core of our beings and consciousness is the core. I can still feel it. With these creatures, you just sense that something is there stirring in awareness. Animals can learn, they remember, they can change their behavior based on new knowledge, all of which may show a mind or intelligence functioning of some sort. And 'in my book' the mind with its dictionary definition written as 'human consciousness,' comes close to 'consciousness.' So I think as I am aware of myself and aware that I exist, that the animals may have a similar awareness. They certainly seem to. I am 'mind-ful' and they may be too. And if they have consciousness, which I think they do, try to go beyond that and imagine all our individual consciousness coming together in a grand merger of infinite measure. This universal consciousness is a source of kinetic energy or living force that we can connect with and tap into to expand our own. Deepak Chopra says "We are all connected through pure consciousness."

And now the $64,000 question: Does consciousness survive when the body dies? People who have had near-death experiences or NDE's, and I know many, all say that after they died their consciousness was alive, left their body and expanded to a mind-blowing (my phrase), surreal awareness. They joined the universal consciousness; a state of clarity and knowing that was far beyond what they had experienced on earth. I believe them and their experience and I wonder what mine will be. Maybe it will be a surprise of huge proportion! Though I know many who think the curtains close for all time when our bodies are deceased and that our consciousness dies with it. The body decays and changes form as in the Bible's 'dust to dust.' But a caveat again; how can conscious energy not, by physics laws, transform into another form or expand its own? No less than Albert Einstein said, "Energy cannot be created or destroyed, it can only be changed from one form to another."

When I was around twelve I remember baby-sitting for the Shanklin family on their farm in Wisconsin. So, as the little baby was having a nap in his bedroom crib, I stood alone and in the quiet of the farm, in front of the living room mirror, I just looked and looked at myself. First seeing my budding breasts show a slight rounded shape under my blouse, I thought "who am I, what is me," and then looking deeper and deeper into my reflection and into my own imagining—"who really is this, am I real, what is going on in this person I see" and "who is me or am I not me and not real" and "Am I really here and seeing me?" Maybe it was a classic philosophic yearning for identity of a pre-pubescent girl, but I remember it vividly to this day. I wanted to know if a 'me' existed and who and what it was. It was a William James moment of some insight, reflected in his definition of consciousness—"awareness of oneself in the world during waking moments."

That childhood awareness has taken me on an amazing journey of searching and sometimes finding. Consciousness is the thing I wonder about most.

DISAPPOINTMENT

January 2014

Way back in the sixth century AD in India a yogic tradition called *Tantra* took hold with stories of goddesses filling the mythological books of the Vedas and the Puranas, the basis of Hinduism. One of the many goddesses was given the name of Dhumavati. She reigned and still does as the *Goddess of Disappointment and Letting Go*. Not as much attention in the form of adoration, worship and her name being invoked was paid to her as to some other goddesses like Lakshmi for abundance and good fortune, Durga for protection and inner strength and the ancient muse Sarasvati for inspiration in all music, poetry, drama and science.

Dhumavati might pale before these and other well-worshipped goddesses, with the word *disappointment's* hurtful import, but she packs a wallop of emotions that load our pathways. People avoid her and yet she daily occupies our thoughts. Worshipers stay away from her because she is not attractive. You can see sadness and failure in her wrinkled face. Her hair is disheveled and she represents things that most people would reject. People do not want to face up to their disappointments, losses and let-downs in life, even though we could learn from them. The goddess could show us all the things that disappoint: other people, faded dreams, failing strength, luck running out and reputation lost. It could fill a lifetime. And then comes the dawn that she also bestows gifts: lessons to be learned, emptiness and detachment to set us on a path of higher awareness. There is wisdom to be found in the most difficult circumstances if we look for it and strength to tap into when our hopes fall away. Look at your worst fears, Dhumavati would say, face your losses and a sage may emerge. That is when real freedom comes. Look lovingly at disappointment and feel love and realize your power. Her wisdom fifteen centuries ago might have come from a modern sage. So I'll say it. *Disappointment is universal* and has been going on for as long as humans have put words to papyrus or bark or a stick writing in the sand. We humans have it in us, innately, to be let down and disappointed! Her message is not just an ancient message but hits home today for vulnerable psyches of all ages and places. And today's experience is not a new phenomenon by any stretch of time.

In our modern culture we don't think about the word *disappointment* much but it carries a lot of weight and it impacts our lives a lot more than you might think. We hear it and feel it often. We say it—"I'm disappointed," "She disappointed me" and "It was a disappointment" over and over. Chances are that it affects our lives every day. If we're not able to do or complete or get or go where we want or something doesn't work out or we want something, expect something and do not get it, or people do things you don't like and don't do things you had hoped for, we're disappointed.

To illustrate this pervasive notion of let-down I have two real life stories that just happened simultaneously in the same past weeks to my grandson and also to me. Both experiences are a bit esoteric, but if you can bear with their surreptitious and convoluted nature, there is a message at the end to make something good of disappointment. On a scale of psychic pain, these were small compared to many in life, but they were disappointments, none the less. And in my stories, we keep an Indian connection to the Hindu sages and goddesses of yesteryear with both my grandson and my present day love of Indian food.

My 26 year old grandson, an analytical mathematician and engineer with a start-up company, spent several weeks in his spare time designing and constructing an over seven foot long 'toy' out of wood. The 'toy' was really a masterful invention for make-believe combat in the world of cyberspace. He was creating a solid, real-life object that you see with your naked eye, can put your hands on, bend and shift around with moving parts and even lick if you wanted. It provokes all the senses. In the tradition of his grandfather Carl (my husband until his death in 1997) who possessed a genius knack for bringing disparate parts together and seeing the whole of the workings of almost anything, my grandson can recognize and 'see' in his mind's eye complex geometric, mathematical formulas and structures and understand and know intuitively how they look and work. All the lines, spaces, surfaces, faces, angles, dimensions and the all-important numbers that come together in any medium, such as wood, he plays with, just for the fun of it, with not necessarily a practical goal in mind. And appropriately, he is building this object in his grandfather Carl's workshop with Carl's tools. As it was taking shape, it had the makings and machinations of something out of this world. His creative juices were flowing. But unbeknownst, lying ahead was a huge disappointment. A meticulous paint job went awry. While Eric was about to encounter his own frustration, I was struggling with mine.

A long time ago, in 1993, I had a show *Crystalline Variations* of twenty-two antique glass sculptures, using flat glass to make three-dimensional, abstract objects, on exhibit in an art gallery on Riverside Drive in New York City. In my research leading to my creations, I saw the beauty of minerals growing into crystal formations and could imagine the colors and shapes inspiring my work in glass. That led to my building sculptures (with Carl's help) of crystals out of glass, each one with the name of a crystal and, with an artist's caveat, I called them Variants. Names such as Staurolite Variant, Cassiterite Variant, Chrysoberyl Variant, Anglesite Variant, Magnesite Variant, Powelite Variant, Zincite Variant and Thenardite Variant filled the spacious Treasure Room Gallery. It was a success with many of the works sold on the spot.

Twenty years later, no longer working in glass but writing books and essays, I wanted to look back and explore the geometric considerations of those sculptures I had built so long ago; that is the mathematical names or the geometric pattern or the 3-D geometric objects with names such as octahedron, tetrahedron, cube and pentagon, and to write about them. In creating my sculptures I was inspired by the crystalline formations in nature, but I hadn't really studied to know the many kinds of mathematical, geometric shapes that manifested in those crystalline variations of my making. So I dug up those names; octahedron, tetrahedron, cube and pentagon, and a lot more 3D shapes in the annals of mathematics including hexagonal pyramid, tetrahedron, icosahedron and octagonal prism to begin to figure out what name or names might apply to what sculpture.

DODECAHEDRON is the name I wanted to focus on. From my reading and research I thought it was the mathematical name for my Fluorite Variant sculpture (two cubes intersecting each other) in 1993 with pardon the pun, some variation. Dodecahedron also was a 'D' word, in my alphabetized listing of words that I wanted to use for an essay in this book as a 'vehicle' to describe geometric shapes and their relation to my crystalline glass sculptures. After days of hunting, writing a mathematics professor and then asking my grandson his opinion, his conclusion was, counter to mine, that my Fluorite sculpture was called Triacontakaihexahedron, a 36-sided polyhedron. I still argued otherwise, considering that there is an illusion in my sculpture (now gracing the New York sunny bedroom of my dear friend Jane for the past three decades), of a continuous straight line, an imaginary line cut through the insides of the two intersecting cubes that would cut down the 36 sides to 12. A dodecahedron has 12 sides, but they are *pentagon* sides. My Fluorite does *not* have pentagon sides. I argued further that there are exceptions to the writings—there are dodecahedrons with four sides to a surface that I saw as examples in books. But finally I conceded. Perhaps the D word for this very same essay should have been DEBATE! *Triacontakaihexahedron* my sculpture was and is.

The evidence for the correct name was strongly in Eric's favor. Though it might seem like a small thing to you, I admit to having a feeling of great disappointment. I had done a lot of work for what? To write about another 'D' word? To not be satisfied totally with the conclusion? To have my heart set on writing about *dodecahedron* and then to let it go? To not be able to describe, at length like I wanted to, the sculptures and their crystal names as well as their 3-D mathematical names (if I could uncover them), in the context of *dodecahedron*? Names and numbers are important to explore! But I had to give up and feel the disappointment of loss.

Meanwhile Eric didn't know what to do. His paint job, so precisely and carefully done by his high standards, had been botched. And hurting even more is that he was following the guidelines of paint strips. They did him in by tearing paint off the edges of his work. Disappointment reigned and chafed.

We were both disappointed. And, remarkably it happened at the same time. Our experiences intersected in early January. We both could have jumped ship and given up. But disappointment led him to contemplate, re-sand, rebuild and restore his work to meet his exact standards with preciseness and precision—his modus operandi. He had the fortitude after a while of lying low and a time of consideration and rest to let new ideas surface and then to resume the work to near perfection. And it is playtime again!

Disappointment of my own led me to think further and harder and to realize the disappointment and admit it. It's not a bad thing to feel bad! And then, I was ready to start over and use the 'D' word thrown in my lap—DISAPPOINTMENT! And I could still write about faces, edges and geometric shapes like I had wanted to do.

When disappointment pervades after much labor to create, in order for you to make things better and feel less anxious, just decide to continue the journey, go on the ride, take the trip through even more days of research and trial and then amazing things can happen. Things open up, a new idea snaps into view, an awareness forms in your thoughts, a kernel of truth shows itself during a pause and it can set you on a new path. Make something good of what we can so easily perceive as bad. Live and face the disappointment. Because, with disappointment comes the wonderful gift of opportunity! It's a chance to learn and explore something else that you might not have searched out. LET GO the Goddess says and move on when the spirit moves.

Eric and I both admitted our disappointments simultaneously and serendipitously did our weekly 'eat out Indian' at the same time.

So tonight, a Sunday on January 12th, we went to the *Mint* in Chapel Hill. We ate our samosas, Chana masala and vegetable korma, all made for vegetarians like we both are. We shared our stories, broke past our disappointments and made a celebration of our breakthroughs, moving on to possibly greater heights.

When stopping in Eric's apartment tonight after the *Mint*, I saw the centerpiece of his bedroom possessions. When he was a college student he visited Canada and helped a class with a science project using Popsicle sticks. Separately, he showed them how to construct

3D geometric shapes out of the wooden Popsicle sticks and glue. Ever since, he has kept a storehouse of those sticks and made 'hedrons' of all sorts. The one that is bigger than a basketball, which survived the years intact and was looking elegant as a sculpture gracing his room, was my nemesis *and* friend, *dodecahedron*! It is one geometric 3-D form of many other structures in nature (Try icy snow! It can form crystals of hollow hexagonal prisms and a prism is a polyhedron.) that I came upon on my own many years ago.

With all these coincidences, intersections and interfaces of happenings and the persuasive calls for attention that *dodecahedron* has presented to me, I submit and will accept the invitations and, of all the 'hedrons' nature has curiously designed, I will call it my own. The *disappointment* of not headlining DODECAHEDRON in this essay led to my 'letting go' and moving on. The journey has taken me to remarkable places. Via the Indian connection, I've traveled with the sixth century Dhumavati, the Hindu Goddess of Disappointment, to the present day eating Indian with Eric and it has been a pleasure! There is no *debate* about things working out in the end.

As I was finishing this essay, with crystal sculptures still on my mind, came another connection out of the blue, bizarre and not yet sorted out by my neural pathways. My Thai massage therapist happened to drop in on a consignment shop along a highway in Durham, selling artistic and household treasures. In the large, meandering space, filled with objects to invite as in a packed old museum, she spotted a glass sculpture up high on a shelf. There in the front on a plaque was my name with the name of the sculpture 'Titanite.' She told me about finding my name and my work. With a hunt I found the store and the sculpture and sat in a chair looking up at it in amazement. Here I was writing about my sculptures and one from my long-past showed up. My thoughts were of Carl, who assisted me in making it. I imagined him soldering that piece and those thoughts were precious thoughts and the work that I hadn't seen in twenty plus years and had no idea until now where it was on the planet, was beautiful. No disappointment here! And I'll call that the last chapter or last paragraph as the case may be. But maybe there will be more to the story…for another day.

P. S. I did buy the sculpture and brought it home.

ELEPHANT

December 2013

A background check, covering millions of years, reveals that *elephantidae* is the only surviving family of the order *proboscidea*. Other families of that order are extinct. Those famous extinct families were the mammoths and the mastodons. Precursors, they were, of our modern day elephant and living from 30 million years ago until they became extinct 10,000 years ago. The mammoths and mastodons roamed the earth together. Imagine that! They looked a lot like modern day elephants but they had their differences too, just as humans might have resembled an early humanoid almost 4 million years ago or looked like Neanderthal Man, an early human, 130,000 years ago. What a history for both the elephant and the human of our genetic heritage over millions of years and of what we survived, how we've evolved and what we have become. Which brings us up to the present day and to our status on the family tree. Or more inclusively and broadly, our status in the biological classification of organisms into groups or *taxa*, based on shared descent from our nearest common ancestor.

Inherent in defining a *family* of life is to consider what makes that family different from other groupings. A collection and listing is made by scientists called taxonomists, of the features and traits that members of the family share in common as well as those inherited from common ancestors. Thus a whole category is made that is unique and unto itself.

In biological classification, let's go back to the earliest grouping of organisms called life. Then continue on down through *kingdom, phylum, class* and *order*, each group with their own common traits. After *order*, a *family* is born in the labs and tomes of science. A definition has been made. And when you settle on your family—take *elephantidae*—you can make an even further breakdown of differences that lead to smaller groupings of similarities known as *genus* and *species*.

Humans are filtered through the same groupings of biological classification as elephants are, leading down to a family called *Hominidae*. We humans and the elephant are together as members of the same first five groups of biological classification. Both the dear elephant and I, to get personal about this, belong to life. We are both alive and kicking. Our shared *kingdom* is animal. Our mutual *phylum* is Chordata. *Mammal* is the class we are both in. *Order* is where we diverge. The elephant is of the *order* Proboscidea. The *order* of humans is Primates. Elephants also have different *genus* and *species* than humans. An elephant's genus is Loxodonta for African elephants and Elephas for Asian ones. Their *species* and full scientific name is Loxodonta Africana for African elephants and Elephas maximus for the Asian elephant. Humans are of *genus* Homo and of the *species* sapiens for a scientific name of Homo sapiens.

So, high up in the rankings of categories, elephants and humans are the same. When we hit *order* we diverged and continued to be separate through the rest of the rankings—*family, genus* and *species*. At the same time as each group is split into smaller groups—e.g. the larger grouping of *class* where both elephant and human are mammal—and then splitting into a still smaller grouping *family* where elephants and humans are different, the entities or organisms within the smaller group are more and more alike. All of the entities in *family* have more in common than the entities in *order*. So, halfway through the biological classification list of eight groups is where we and the elephants show our differences. But the half above is where elephants and humans are similar and of like kind.

It is the sameness we share, the being 'in tune with' that I love about the elephant. We have traits in common by scientific measure and I have my own speculations of the amazing connection and good vibrations I feel when I'm with the largest living terrestrial animal on earth. Simpatico! It is our sharing of traits, their reaching out to connect, our working to understand them and learning from them—no animal is too small (I jest!) to teach us a thing or two—that I am writing this essay about.

Their consciousness comes first in importance for me. And it permeates all their other aspects and characteristics that we admire and maybe aspire to and that we both have in common to varying degrees. I think they are conscious beings, though there are still skeptics in the world of science.

The immediate and inevitable thing to know on meeting an elephant for the first time, whether you're the proverbial blind man feeling his way around the unknown life form or the infant catching an impression in a zoo, is this. It is huge! It can be up to 29 feet long, 13 feet high to the shoulder and weigh up to 15,000 pounds. It holds the record as the biggest of all living, terrestrial animals and is so strong that, unlike all other creatures in the animal kingdom, it hardly needs to defend itself. It intimidates any possible aggressor with its size and strength. Potential predators such as lions, tigers, hyenas and wild dogs tend to keep their distance and usually target only the young elephants or calves. Protecting their young is one thing that brings out the elephant's aggression. They roar and run and mock charge, which all create seismic signals heard at great distances, and the sound brings the herd together. The seismic waveforms produced by locomotion travel up to 20 miles through the ground and the waveforms of vocalizations travel through the air for 10 miles. The impact of the signals is strong and widespread. Some of their vocalizations are infrasonic that are waves or vibrations with frequencies below that of audible sound. Their communication systems are impressive.

With the threat of predators, the family group packs tight to protect their young. Their big ears are stretched out to look even bigger, their heads are raised and they lash out with their tusks if necessary, while protecting their trunks. They are smart enough to know that trunks are too valuable to risk injury. They stand tall and big. Size matters for the impressions it makes.

As a human I admire showing strength. Be strong and confident in your actions and in the picture you present to others. I can avoid any disturbing, verbal confrontation by having a surety of mind. And, like the elephant that makes a show of strength to protect her young, what you project might protect you from further aggression. Growing up with a pacifist's mentality, I am one to quickly get away from the hits and punches at almost all costs. Physical aggression is not in my make-up but, like the elephant, if push comes to shove and I have to do something to save my life and my children I would probably fight back in some fashion. I respect the elephant's restraint *and* actions.

Their trunk is vital to their survival. It is a fusion of the nose with the upper lip that occurs after birth and it contains well over 100,000 bundles of muscle. The elephant uses it like we would our arms and fingers, but the trunk contains little fat and no bone. Imagine it as a very long nose. Elephants use their trunks to breathe, smell up to two miles away, touch, grasp, suck water up to two gallons worth and then spray it into their mouth, make sounds and lift up to 800 pounds. The Asian elephant has one and the African elephant has two finger-like projections at the end of the trunk to grasp objects for delicate tasks, like we do with opposing thumb and fingers.

Their sounds made through the larynx and assisted by the trunk, include babbling when an infant, bellowing when hurt and rumbling when aroused. They grunt and snort through their trunks to talk to each other. They raise their trunks above their heads and trumpet loudly in great excitement and to scare off aggressors. There is much to research and learn about what they are saying.

We families, E*lephantidae* and *Hominidae*, spend about the same number of years on this earth—70 to 80 years. Our normal body temperature is virtually the same—97'F elephant and 98.6'F human. Our heads and craniums are large, especially in the elephant to accommodate muscles that hold up the neck and skull and the weight of the large brain and ears. The males are larger than the females. Elephants usually have 26 teeth and most humans have 32. The elephant's tusks are modified upper-jaw incisors. Humans are right or left-handed. Elephants are right or left-tusked. We share a mostly right dominance. We both have ear flaps but theirs are much bigger and more useful to flap and cool off and shoo away insects. The big African elephant's ears are shaped like the continent of Africa. They hear at lower frequencies so we are not aware of their very active communication for miles of sound travel. But they hear at our range, also, to know of any threats. I am thinned skin compared to their up-to one inch thick, gray, wrinkled hide. Mud is their sunscreen against ultra-violet light on very sensitive skin. They, but not me, can swim up to 30 miles at a stretch, using their trunk as a snorkel (lucky for them!). They inhale air mostly through the trunk.

They have pretty much the same sexual organs as humans do, including a clitoris, vulva, testes and a very long penis that reaches up to 39", with a diameter of 6" at the base. Plus, the elephant has a temporal gland in both sides of the head, a unique organ for both females and males that releases fluid affecting sexual behavior. Females are fertile up to about 50 years of age, like humans. They have from one to three offspring and rarely have twins. Pregnancy lasts almost two years but the baby comes out nearly ready to stand up and walk. All the elephants gather round to touch and caress the newborn with their trunks and legs. It is touching to see their trunks and legs entwining in photographs. The elephant touch is a comfort to them in finding out about their world. Human babies enjoy a similar welcome to the world with love and attention. The elephant mother stays closely attentive to give their baby protection from predators and to provide nutrition. That includes two to four months of breast feeding and two to four years of suckling. And all the while, they are searching for vegetation and teaching their young to do the same. Some young calves suck on their trunks, just as human babies suck their thumbs. That's another image that makes for a strong elephant-human connection.

They play. And it comes with side benefits, learning coordination and social skills. It is a glorious time of youth for most mammals including us. Females run or chase each other and males play-fight. Hormones are at work in both elephant and human families. At around nine to twelve years of age the female elephant matures sexually, ahead of the males maturing when they hit their teens. As in humans, the girls also are ahead of the boys. Around this time, when the young males begin to fight and try to mate, the mothers chase the males away from their tight-knit matriarchal family groups or herds (averaging 10 members) and the males join other males in other places or they go-it alone. As humans we can relate to that time of life as parents or as teens, though it is less likely, but still possible, that we would make the males leave home.

Like me, elephants are herbivorous. That is one of my attractions to their family. They don't kill other animals for food, like most animals do. They co-exist peacefully with other herbivores, for the most part. They eat leaves, bark, twigs, fruit and roots; 300+ pounds of it per day. Elephants can be browsers and/or grazers depending on the terrain they dwell in. They stay near or move to their water holes to be able to each drink up to 60 gallons a day. Just like us, they eat three meals a day. And like some of us, they take an afternoon nap, but standing, under the shade of trees. At night they sleep lying down. To keep meeting their own demands for resources, they move up to 12 miles a day or more, making seasonal migrations in search of food, water and mates. While moving from place to place the family of mostly females with a matriarch leading the group might connect with another family to form a *bond group* and they may or may not cluster to a *clan*. They do not form a strong bond with these larger groups but as a group they can defend feeding and water ranges from other clans. Humans have their own form of bond groups and clans, you name it. Sociability and strength in numbers are benefits for both the elephant and the human. Researchers think that the high sociability of elephants adds to their intelligence which is legendary.

And here is yet another thing to be impressed with. Elephants have shown remarkable intelligence. Their brains are the biggest, at up to 13 pounds (human brains weigh four pounds), of any land animal and it is highly complex. Their superior intelligence can be shown by the structure of the brain. Studies show that the neocortex of the elephant is highly convoluted, as is our brain. Theirs' shows a gyral pattern full of brain folds that may be more complex than ours. The convolutions are an indicator of complex intelligence. Elephants have a large and highly convoluted hippocampus that is bigger even than that of a human. The volume of the cerebral cortex (the locale of cognition) exceeds that of any primates, and that be us!

And for cognitive ability in making and using tools, an elephant can modify a branch to use as a flyswatter, even without having arms. With intention and concentration (I've seen the videos), they can paint a picture with a paintbrush and with one elephant, a painting of an elephant! How is that for a sense of self? They show learning for behavior and new facts and then remember them years later, they can mimic, show altruism and cooperation and use language consisting of body language and vocal sounds. They have long memories for territory and are able to keep track of where their family members are. They recognize elephants they haven't seen in years—witness their excitement and animation on seeing them, as in an emotional reunion between two old friends.

As for emotions, elephants are famous in literature, art and science laboratories. They exude joy when they meet. They care for each other. They show compassion. A matriarch will put herself at risk and face down poachers while the rest of her family escapes. They give support to the dying. They grieve for the dead. They remember the bones of family members and friends that they come upon in their travels and they smell, stroke and lift the bones with their trunks. And they spend hours and days in their meditation on the bones and in contemplation. Yes, I mean that they contemplate; the word which brings me to consciousness.

Some scientists are still wary of ascribing that esoteric but all-encompassing word to any animal. There is not enough evidence for them or they just can't handle the word itself, even though it's been around for centuries. But the elephants have such irrefutably, remarkable abilities, that I see consciousness, as I said early on in the essay, permeating all aspects of the elephant that we admire, aspire to and have in common.

A lot of the abilities, skills and actions that the elephants display, I think, come out of self-awareness. That's the jackpot. Here's some evidence. Elephants recognized themselves in mirrors in a study that John Roach reported on for National Geographic News, October 30, 2006. The tests revealed behaviors that we recognize as behavior of self-recognition in a mirror. That is *self-awareness*. Consciousness is awareness of ourselves. We know that elephants lead socially complex lives and display empathy, concern and understanding of another's feelings. And Joshua Plotnik, a graduate student in 2006 in psychology at Emory University said, "There seems to be some correlation between an ability to recognize oneself in a mirror and higher forms of social complexity," The elephant sees itself as separate from others. That's the news.

I saw a video recently of a small group of elephants in Thailand listening to Paul Barton play his piano out on the compound grass. One of the elephants named Peter came up close behind Paul and whipped his trunk under his own chest to gain a swinging momentum and then swung it forward to hit the lower piano keys. Peter did it again and again with an occasional deliberate swing to the top of Paul's head and held the end of his trunk there like a plunger with suction. Then he swung his trunk back and forth to hit the keys again. While Paul and Peter kept playing, a neighboring elephant, Soi, turned back to face the crowd of elephants and shifted his ample hips back and forth in a wiggle dance to the rhythm of the music and he kept it up. Peter and Soi seemed to be having a joyous time and were certainly in tune with Paul's music and in pitch for a colloquy of harmony.

That's what I imagine with the elephant. A close connection solidified. We're neighbors on the family tree. We want to learn from you and know what we don't know about you. You are a picture of mystery and intrigue.

We do know that it has been a tough, rough life for you when humans have gotten into the picture. You're an object of display in zoos—but how else will we see you? Hard-driving humans have turned you into work-elephants, like work-horses through centuries of time and you have not always been treated well. Long ago you were forced to fight in wars alongside human warriors, though you did not share the cause whatever it was—to gain more territory, to be rid of humans of lesser pedigree or to find freedom from oppressors. You would have wanted your own freedom in the wild. You've been trained for circus performances to show off your talents and you had to comply to avoid the pain inflicted on you. Humans have suffered similar insults and been on the receiving end of a lot of bad treatment, too, which doesn't speak well for some in the human race. We Homo sapiens have that pain in common with you Loxodonta Africanas and Elephas maximus. We can empathize and should know better. We may be of different genus and species to spice up our lives and at the same time we have so much in common to keep us together.

As for the destruction of the forests in which you live and in the poaching for your ivory that is killing thousands of elephants every year, we ask of you to please, as spoken in the Lord's Prayer, *Forgive us our trespasses*. You, dear elephants, have been guileless in the rampage to supply the world with ivory, especially China for medicines. We desperately want your family to hang around in the wild for eons to come. We'd only be hurting ourselves by losing you.

Aristotle, the ancient Greek philosopher, said that elephants were "The animal which surpasses all others in wit and mind." His lifetime was from 384-322 BC, twenty-four hundred years ago, and what he said is still golden today. You're a treasure beyond measure.

Yes, Peter and Soi and all the other elephants out there. We could use some of your elephant wisdom in keeping a rich, peaceful, long-lasting life going for all.

FOOD and FASTING

February 2014

Welcome to Barmecide's feast! Imagine all the foods that meet your needs and desires. They are spread out in abundance on the table before you. It is truly a feast for the eyes. But there is more to it than meets the eye. As in the *Arabian Nights* where the rich man serves a beggar an imaginary banquet, much is promised but nothing is delivered. All the lush, colorful, aromatic and sensuous food is a product of the imagination. It's an illusion. There is really nothing at all to eat. But the beggar plays along (and you can too). And there is always some truth to fiction and fiction to fact.

Long ago across the land of the Holy Roman Empire and spilling over into Egypt and Syria, from at least a thousand years BC to the third century AD and beyond, lived ascetics practicing to the glory of their gods. They deprived themselves of anything that gave them pleasure, such as a roof over their heads, shoes on their feet, money, baths, sexual ecstasy, body rest and food. Though they might have imagined a rich bounty of breads and soups and honey, they lived life without attachments. Of all the ascetic practices that spread across religions and regions, fasting was the most common and is still practiced today. The ancient Greeks fasted. The Christians fasted during lent for 40 days. The Muslims, following the prophet Muhammad, fasted through the month of Ramadan and the dervishes and fakirs of Sufi had times of fasting according to religious calendars. But it was the die-hards—the ascetics, saints, monks and hermits of these religions—that were known for intense, ruthless and unrelenting fasting. Some were even known to not drink water. But oxygen filled the lungs without let up until their bodies expired. They practiced extreme fasting even though it was and is common knowledge that air, water and food are the three essential things that living forms need to keep chemical processes going and thus to keep us alive. It was as if they were daring the gods to keep them alive with heavenly light. as trees feed on the sun and water in photosynthesis.

Two words describe this extreme fasting or famishment: *inedia* and *breatharianism*. Inedia is defined as the ability to live without food. Breatharianism is a belief system with followers who say food is not necessary. They claim that humans can be sustained solely by prana or vital life force and that this nutritional energy can be converted from sunlight and even moonlight. Yogis are written about that live only on holy breath or air. Some adherents fast for many months, although medics say that generally only a couple of months without food is survivable. And there have been tales through the ages of the ascetics never eating food for years on end. How is that possible? The reality is that fats, proteins and carbohydrates are the necessary sources of energy for the body and your body cannot make them. You need to consume calories to produce energy and calories come from food or fuel as in a car engine. In the extended absence of caloric intake the body burns its own reserves of glycogen, body fat and muscle (though the Breatharians say you do not consume those reserves while fasting). Not eating leads to starvation, dehydration and eventual death. I have read of people having no food for years but there is always some hitch. Like a fasting monk only having the Eucharist (bread is food and wine is water!) or a Jainist occasionally having buttermilk (that is a complete food unto itself!). The ones who claim to never consume food are found to make exceptions. That little bit of something is what might make the difference to keep them alive. And, in more recent decades, attempts to study them scientifically seem to fall on misinformation, inaccuracies and lack of fool-proof and scholarly research. How do you set up a research project where people are starving themselves, possibly to death? I guess you measure the changes in a body up to a point and then stop the study.

I suggest, if only we could be like a plant! With photosynthesis, we could turn that light force, that holy light into chemical energy to be stored and released to fuel our bodies. As a bonus, oxygen is generally released as a waste product of photosynthesis which could feed our vital body processes! Is this the inexplicable, mysterious gift of the mystics who eat no food and maybe drink no water but claim to survive on light? Do they have something resembling photosynthesis that comes alive in their bodies when deprived and the circumstances demand it? Is anything possible?

It is time to put eating back in play and to modify the extreme fasting regimen because there are benefits. Drinking vegetable juices is one kind of modified fast. I do it. There are good reasons to fast. It helps clear out the toxins. It gives the digestive track a rest and allows for healing, if necessary, to take place. It clears the head with the spare impact that a fast has on the body. It super nourishes the body with a rich supply of minerals and enzymes. My dad, Arvid, used to fast regularly with nothing but water for perhaps a week or so. He felt fine and then returned to his usual good food and died at age 81 in 1971.

He set an example for me to fast as a practice, but my fasting is not as extreme as his. Every several months I go on a week-long fast of my own making to clean out my system and to give it a rest. I drink juices during the fast and lots of water, but I do not eat solid food. The juices are mostly organic vegetables and greens and to a lesser extent fruits. I buy and drink ready-made fresh juices aa well as dried powder of greens shaken up with water. I also put vegetables and plenty of water in a blender (which means I am getting some pulp). I used to use a juicer (which meant no pulp) but it is too much work. Food can be a lot of work! I make sure that I keep up all my regular exercise activities which include walking daily, chi gong and yoga, lifting weights and I meditate for any length up to an hour a day. The rest of the day I give to my projects and to people. I do not feel faint, I have high energy and I imagine all the good affects. One could keep this up way longer than a week but one week is enough for me and I go back to good solid food. You do need food but it should be good food and most people have some idea of what that means.

My good solid food includes lots of raw and some cooked vegetables, whole grains of bread, oatmeal and amaranth, nut butters—especially sunflower seed butter without added sugar, olive and coconut oil for the brain, dairy butter, occasional eggs and a little cheese, some raw fruits, a cookie with no or little sweetener and if so I use honey or agave sparingly (I don't like much sweet) and as a special treat frozen rice dream. To spice things up and for health benefits I use turmeric, cinnamon and red hot chili powder. I don't consume alcohol, sugar or caffeine and the few supplements I take are mostly concentrated food, as in whole beet tablets or garlic tablets. That's pretty much it in a nutshell for my diet. And I feel good and healthy and packed with energy. We do need nutrients but not a lot of calories unless you are exercising, walking, running, lifting weights or have a physically demanding career such as a construction job. But there are still only so many calories that we need. You know you are consuming too many calories when the fat starts piling on.

To handle the digestion of all this good food I want to give special credit where credit is due. The **liver** wins the prize for its amazing work. It is the chemical factory of your body. For all that the nutrients like protein and fat that our body is not able to make (we can store fat though!), the liver comes through big time. After our good food is digested through the mouth, stomach and intestines, with byway influences of the pancreas and gall bladder, it is absorbed into the bloodstream and moves on to the liver. There the digested food ingredients are made into new components, each liver cell being a highly complex factory making thousands of new compounds every second. Its tasks are many! The liver helps to control blood sugar levels. The liver filters toxic substances out of your blood. It breaks down and recycles blood cells to keep up with the two million new red blood cells that the bone marrow (mainly in the femur) produces EVERY SINGLE SECOND! The liver releases stored glucose when necessary. It converts simple substances from our digestive system into way more complex molecules that can be transported by the blood stream to every living cell in the body. The liver is the only organ in the body that can regenerate itself. That says something about its magnificence! For all the good things it does for me I try to treat it well.

Yeah for our amazing liver! And applause for our eating highly nutritious, vitamin and mineral loaded (to feed our very own chemical factory) organic, toxic-free food to make the digestive trip without detours, as in having to filter out toxins. We do not want to overload our systems with poisons. They can lead to death and alcohol and drugs, both legal and illegal, are a big culprit! And do not overtax the body with the organ work of digesting too much food. Our body needs way less food than most people eat in order to not build up a lot of fat storage, which is a stress and a burden to carry around. Help the liver to keep our body processes functioning optimally and to provide fuel for energy. Try it! You might like it!

And let's face it. Food or the lack of it can be the source of good and bad. Food can be a lot of pleasure and a life-sustaining support. It can also inflict a lifelong challenge with overconsumption or under consumption, with addiction and anorexia, health issues with extra weight, and be a suspect with accompanying toxins and poisons in causing cancer and an array of other diseases and maladies and, at the same time, a seeming cure (without the toxins) for that same array. It can be a welcome solace for the psyche and an ancient and legendary aphrodisiac like almonds for fertility and passion, radish as a turn-on and pomegranate to lift up testosterone levels for sexual pleasure. But, delving into all that is for another day and book!

I'll give my health conscious dad the last word. "You are what you eat," I heard him say hundreds of times, as well as this, "And those are the facts."

GRANDMA with GRACE

December 2013

Dear Asher, Erickson, Lauren, Isaac, Isabella, Melia and Kai,

I am writing to you with the end of the year 2013 fast approaching. Thanksgiving has passed and Christmas is on the way. Both are traditional times of giving and receiving and saying thank you to others for our many gifts. We all have a lot to be grateful for and that is why I am writing this letter to each of you, dear grandchildren. You have thanked me for many things through the years and I have thanked you. But it's time for me to thank you all at once with a longer and more profound expression of my love.

The most important thing for me is that you each were born! You were conceived in the most wonderful and miraculous of ways with loving parents, you grew inside a safe, warm place and, when you were ready you came into this world and graced us with your being. What an incredible event for each of you! Your moms 'gave birth' to precious you. It was a gift of a lifetime for all of us! We are glad you are here.

Asher and Erickson grew to be eleven years old and nine years old when your dear grandfather, Carl, died. That was such a sad and difficult time for you. He did so many things with you that you remember. He took you Asher on a car trip up the east coast to see historical sights and he made another car trip west from North

Carolina with Erickson to New Mexico. He made toys with you in his workshop. You still miss him, I know. I think you know that he influenced you in many wonderful ways and helped you to be good people and to accomplish things with your special talents. You Lauren were only nine months old when you lost your grandfather. But I'm so glad that he knew you and you knew him. I helped you to remember him with pictures and you did.

It is such good fortune that you three had a little bit of knowing him. All the things that one wants a grandfather to be, he was. Kind, sweet and loving and he spent time with you. What a gift!

The rest of you do feel like you knew him, with all that I have told you about him and I still do today when the right occasion arises. I want you to have that knowledge as your heritage. We talk about him like he is in our lives now. Thank you, wonderful children, for taking all of that into your minds and hearts to carry through your lifetimes.

You dear souls add up to seven, God's perfect number in the Bible and my number, too. How special that is! Seven of you were born to my three children and their spouses. Try that number on for size. When I leave this earth, maybe someone of you will carry on with favoring 'seven.' It's another heritage I can pass on.

Grandmothers have a special place in our lives and I'm glad you have me. Some grandchildren never know their grandparents. But we are so lucky. I had a Grandmother Sarah until I was eight years old. She milked the cows, spun yarn for knitting and wove rugs on her big Swedish loom. I played the piano and sang and talked to her to try to make her feel better when she was sick. She was 82 years old when she died. We felt privileged to have her stay with us.

One of the things I have wanted for you is that we make special trips together—just me and one of you at a time. Since Asher is the oldest of you seven, he and I have gone to several places. That includes many states and flying up to Alaska as far as the Arctic

Circle. We saw the Northern Lights! Erickson and I have driven to Florida for a week to join a group looking for UFO's and we have had adventures in other places, like Scrabble and chess tournaments in other states. I've indulged in some pride with your winning several championships. Lauren and I had a beautiful 10 days in Barcelona in 2011. Melia and I went to Spain this past summer of 2013 and toured the whole country. Both you girls could speak some Spanish and I thank you for being my translators! I've taken the rest of you to different places and am planning more trips in times ahead. How lucky I am to have time with each of you alone! Our memory banks are full to draw on when we want to day dream. You are all troopers for travel and I revel in your happiness and enthusiasm. Your fresh young minds jazz up our lives. There is not a chance of growing old. It's because of you.

Our lives at home have been full with times together, too. You come to mine or I go to yours and talk, play games, eat out, see friends and do whatever our hearts desire. I am satiated but am always ready for more!

As the years roll by, I have been blessed with your love, your youthful energy, your excitement for life and it is mutual I know! You've told me that. Wow!

Now, a grandmother holds a special place in different ways in all cultures. I feel that my place has been and will keep being to love and accept you totally for what you are. You are amazing human beings and I am not out to change you. You are your own unique selves, beyond what I might have imagined, and you will evolve and change yourselves as you go on in life. I can pass on ideas, point out people's expectations which don't necessarily have to be your own, but might grease the skids (allow me my youthful but 'old-fashioned' expressions!) for your own journey through life and I can guide you through rough spots if you are open to it. I feel good about setting an example for your living a rich, full life. You have seen what is important to me and I see some of those values blossoming in you. Kindness, thoughtfulness, fun, playfulness and the list goes on.

Just for you to know now and to understand, I'll share some other thoughts I have about the very honored and privileged place I have been fortunate enough to have in your lives, as a grandmother. And you may be grandparents yourselves someday!

If there is any one thing that is called for, any quality that helps most in my being a grandma, I think it is this. Grace. It's not a word you hear much these days. People are sometimes named Grace, but I've known only one and that was in my cradle through high school years. Grace Towner was her name. She lived with her mother as a 'spinster' in a small house in my home town. She never married, had no children and was never a grandmother. I also knew about the word 'grace' from saying 'Grace' in thankfulness before a meal and knowing 'grace' from the Bible and from the hymns we sang in the Baptist church that both our family and Grace Towner and her mother attended. 'But by the grace of God I am what I am;' we quoted from I Corinthians 15:10. We sang 'Amazing grace! how sweet the sound,' with tears in our eyes. Grace Towner seemed to fit that word. She had a quiet, simple dignity about her, nothing flashy, showing forgiveness, in spite of being ill most of her life, and charity left unsaid but felt by me.

Grace is a quality you can feel in the presence of someone. Harmony, agility and dexterous, poise, love and forgiveness all catch the spirit of the word.

As a grandma I am blessed with grace. Whatever happens with you and whatever you do, I feel grace. In all the active things we do together I am flexible and agile as a kid roller skating around the block. Good health abounds and I feel grace in the making. Grace is there to face the losses when we are graced enough to get older.

You've probably read and heard about the wisdom of grandmothers. Well, frankly kids, I shy away from that word. I think we all are wise. I saw it in each of you as a babe taking in the newness of the world. Your perceiving and knowing, at every age and stage of your living and gracing the planet, has been astonishing to me. I have learned life lessons from you in increments more than you might have learned from me. Thank you from the bottom of my heart.

I wish the best for you as you live your lives with vigor, integrity and vibrancy. And with grace. I love you.

Your ever lovin' Grandma

Ethel Erickson Radmer

HOME

January 2013

Submitted to a competition in 2013 on subject of 'Home' and
not awarded any of 3 prizes
With minor changes and additions in 2014

Non-fiction Stream of Consciousness

These high boots are made for walking striped and colored
like a zebra and a new gift from my son. The wild and crazy me
along with a maroon for past hopeful healing shirt and blue tights
that I had when my husband was alive and a newer maroon for
still healing sweater top my daughter gave me. And out to Golden
Corral we go to the place of my husband's last happy Thanksgiving
his face all smiles after a throat dilation that made it possible for
the passage of food. And with that he could swallow like normal
with our youngest from California and all of us so thankful for his
enjoying the feast. He exuded gratefulness. Now this time it is to
remember our dear happy man on January 5th 2013 the day and
time a quarter to noon that he took his last breath sixteen years ago.
Happy Sweet Sixteen Death Day a family member said and we
laughed and our sweet man would have laughed too because we're
that kind of family. Home is where the heart is and our hearts were

together on this. And we felt at home with each other even though our dear man was gone.

Oh I've lived a life before he and I partnered. I was born into a home my place of origin in my mother's bedroom with the doctor attending. A place secure and safe which is what you want your home to be. And it stayed the embracing comforting place that I could count on where I lived until college. I was born to a family filled with love and caring in a home where we were watched over and cherished for who we were. Then it was time to go away from home leave the nest and an empty nest it was for my parents with me being the last of our brood of seven. Off to the University and a career and meeting my mate for over 39 years of for real wedded bliss and having our children and making so warm a home of our own. How firm the foundation was for me with my past. And all through that steadfast deep-rooted lifetime I was more than meets the eye.

I was and am a vagabond at heart. Peripatetic. A traveler moving about from place to place. A loner and at the same time a social butterfly. A seeker who is taken with the mysteries of our existence and on an even grander scale the whole universe and all the space that can be imagined. How is it all here and there? Put me on another habitable planet and that would be home for me and not just in the direction of my earthly home. I would look out further from that planting to an even more confounding magnificence.

Oh yes I've lived a life grounded as a professional woman an occupational therapist a wife a mother of three a grandmother of seven an artist journeying through several media but especially glass a musician of several instruments a writer of several books a glorious life I might add. And firm solid. Like the foundation of a structure you might call home. A place where one can leap away from or sail off to right on target to strike home.

When my husband left home for an unknown place in space I grieved. Where now was the strength of our home together? I plunged deep into my soul for years of learning growth hurts changes and have uncovered what was there all along. My strength is within. The searcher keeps looking and finding. Trailing coursing waving floating over and throughout is the yen the urge to see what's on the other side to know the things I didn't know. The solid core of who I am is thirst a drive a burning curiosity leading to wandering wondering seeing what's in the world and beyond and who else is part of the human species. Wherever and whatever that is or may become is home for me and always was.

My husband's spirit has found I think a home of its own in the grand universe and he has always had a home in my heart. Is there I ask the sixty four thousand dollar question a home beyond for those spirits to exist and to come together? My mother spoke and sang of her heavenly home and to be at home with the Lord after she left this earth. She imagined it, felt the love of an everlasting home with her creator and I believe it was real for her. If you can picture it and feel it that much is real.

But back on earth I'm at home today wherever I am in these zebra boots made for walking, wandering and wondering to the end of my earthly days.

With that essay written but without any prizes have I earned my zebra stripes my son?

Ethel Erickson Radmer

INTERNET

December 2013

Imagine a huge cluster of gossamer tendrils (it's the artist in me) but not delicate; more like a strong cobweb branching out from what looks like a central core. One filament fans out into another branch of threads; each set branching out into more sets of branching to create a mass—possibly a critical mass with the demands made of it, and sending messages in a wavelength beyond the far end of visible light—red—and traveling off the charts, possibly to infinity. It is kind of like a fern but way more extensive and more complex as it keeps spreading out further and further. With electronic equipment, we can detect and measure the signals that are sent over the pathways and trace the route. So our imagining becomes visible. The overall look is beautiful. It could be a drawing on a wall in black and white or a painting in color, if you're inspired to differentiate and highlight the filaments of communication.

What we are seeing is a *global system of interconnected computer networks*. The microfibers that we are drawing and painting are *routing paths*. It is a network of networks with an exalted name, prefaced by a *definite article* for generic force to set it up. The INTERNET.

It crept up on us in the sixties when our government commissioned researchers to build strong communication through computer networks. The United Kingdom and France pitched in and precursor networks were established. This led to the eighties and to private and public funding for developing new network technologies worldwide. It proved useful in business, government and academia and led to the merger of many networks. No one seems able to pin down an exact date in the midst of all this action in the '80's but we know that well before the turn of the century the internet was born. And what an impact around the planet this international network has made! It has been popularized and incorporated into almost every aspect of modern human life.

This revolution has brought along with it a whole new vocabulary. New words were dubbed, old words were given new or expanded meanings.. And the concepts are new. How do we learn all this, I ask, and not even to say, how do we integrate this into our day to day existence? I revel in English and all its nuances. But another new language is not my strong suit.

The computer itself has presented its own challenges to the cortex and in dexterity of thought and action. But, it's been going on for decades now and we're sort of used to it, with accommodations to new systems, software and updates. It's almost old hat.

The truth is that the Internet is not the hurdle that learning to use a computer was for me. But the implications of using it are big.

Just to be clear on terminology. The terms *Internet* and *Worldwide Web* are often used interchangeably as you and I might talk. But there is a difference and we should know it. The *Web*, as abbreviation of *Worldwide Web,* is just one of many services running on the internet. The web is a collection of web pages that are linked by hyperlinks and URLs (uniform resource locators), also commonly known as a *web address*. This makes possible going to a website by using a web address, like finding a friend's home by using his street address. In addition to the web, other services of many dozens that the internet provides include email, file sharing, newsgroups, remote computer control, online games, e-commerce and dial-up access by telephone and telecommunication providers. The supermarket of offerings on this smorgasbord for consumption is huge.

Getting there is simple enough. I double left-click my mouse on my *Mozilla Firefox* icon. Firefox is just one of many web browsers like *Google Chrome, Internet Explorer, Opera* and *Safari*. A news page (set up by my high-techie son-in-law) comes up which indicates that I have landed on the internet. A world of information is waiting for my beckoning

The internet has opened up. My computer has connected to another computer and it could be anywhere in the world using routers and servers. I type in the top left bar a web address or a subject that I want to search or several key words to bring up a list of sites related to my subject request. And I click and click to continue the search. I am navigating my way through a potpourri of offerings.

I'm not alone! Over a third of the seven billion population of the world, that is close to three billion people have hooked into the internet.

The unseen work of maintenance of the internet is done by service providers like Sprint, MCI Worldcom, GTE, ANS, UUNET and AT&T U-verse. In our free market system they are motivated to compete and maintain consistent and fast connections which benefits everyday Internet users and we are them. There is no central governing body of the internet but there is an Internet Engineering Task Force, a non-profit organization, to whom any one of us may contribute technical expertise.

The internet is a pretty free-wheeling place. There is little interference from anyone in authority. Users have fought to keep it that way without government regulation and taxing. Even the most liberal progressive and the conservative republican want to keep the Internet free. It is open and libertarian like the Wild West! So in that one way we are returning to our country's roots instead of making change!

The social impact of the internet is pronounced in every area of our encounters as well as when we are alone. Our way of living and being has altered for all time. There's no going back!

People can work from home so there is flexibility in employment hours and location. Collaborative projects are done more easily on the internet. Educational material for all ages to earn a degree is on web sites with no need to travel to a campus.

Facebook, Twitter and MySpace are all social networking websites that have opened the doors on socializing and interaction. Millions of people use message boards and blogs as a way to share ideas. There are virtual communities at leisure of all ages who enjoy games. Anyone can download music and movies of their choice and see dance, demonstrations of special skills and flash crowds on YouTube.

Lonely people can spend every waking moment using the internet to share their feelings and stories with others and gain comfort. Singles are looking for mates. There are sites to learn of and share medical knowledge for most any disease or health condition you might have and offer support for each other.

Groups raise money through crowdsourcing. Academics share and disperse information beyond their own institutional turf to other countries. Political revolutions and campaigns use the internet as a way to get out the vote, to raise money and organize and give rise to change as we saw practiced by rebels in Egypt during the Arab Spring.

Our time and attention have been redirected. Social gatherings are almost always punctuated with our technology and making virtual connections. The language in email and messaging has become coded and cryptic. Our record keeping is left to the winds, no solid letters here. And all these changes in our networking will only grow bigger and change yet again.

What do we do with this? Cry in our soup? Be an admirer on the sidelines? Feel bad about change? Long for the good old days? Or do we join in and make the most of it? I'll opt for participating with gusto. Let's have a joyful time making waves that we never made before. The internet is there for the offing.

I had just completed this essay and set it aside in December 2013, when I got a phone call from a stranger in the Midwest. She was Chinese and had been searching the internet for any information she could find about her grandfather, whom she had never known. She knew that he had attended a certain school in China. What came up for her was my book, *Walking The Rails: My Childhood in Whitehall.* I had written about this school, the Home of Onesiphorus for Children, and about my aunt and uncle who, as missionaries, helped care for and teach these children without parents, who had been left on the orphanage doorstep. They were the head teachers for a number of years until my Uncle Victor died and my Aunt Marie had completed her mission and returned to the United States. The Chinese woman who called me had known her grandfather's name was Victor and could never figure out why. When she heard about my book on the internet and learned from me that Reverend Victor Carlson, my uncle (before I was born) ran the Home of Onesiphorus for Children and school in the 1920's, she knew. Her orphan grandfather, whose unknown parents probably had dropped him off at the doorstep as a baby or a very young boy had somehow gotten the name Victor after my uncle and the young boy attended the school and it was his home as it was for all the other orphans. The woman who called me, with our mutual sharing, cried to have learned more about her grandfather's roots. We want and need to know about our heritage! I knew my Aunt Marie had many Chinese visitors, a few of whom I may have even met as a very small child, to her home in America for the rest of her life and that the ancestor of the woman who called me was maybe one of them. I may learn even more with my own searching and the Chinese woman and I can talk again. The internet has opened doors beyond our imagining.

JUKEBOX

April 2014

Doris Day, I love you! At age 90 years this month of April you say "I'm positive. I just am. I still feel like the best is yet to come." As one of the biggest box office stars of the 40s and 50s you've had quite a journey in your lifetime. You yourself say it's been full of joy, fun, happiness and health. And to be able to say that is such a gift! Among your many classics of song is *Sentimental Journey*. I loved that song, every word of it, with your cheerful, lilting soprano voice coming out of a beautiful music box in the City Café of my hometown of Whitehall, Wisconsin in the late 1940s and 1950s. That time and place were my roots.

Please, let me take that *Sentimental Journey*—your first #1 hit in 1945 with the greatly missed swingin' Les Brown and His Band of Renown and visit an era in which I grew up. It is the age of the Jukebox. And your *Sentimental Journey* was one of the many discs that had its place in thousands of jukeboxes across the land.

Gonna take a sentimental journey
Gonna set my heart at ease
Gonna make a sentimental journey
To renew old memories

My old memories of the jukebox are as fresh as daffodils in April. How could they not be with such beauty of sight and sound? The colors, oh the kaleidoscope of pink, yellow, red, blue and green, flashing with neon and changing under translucent glass and plastic pilasters and columns fronting and rounding the wood and metal framed box. A large frosted glass panel on the front showed off an etched or screened design motif of deer or birds, swoops and swirls, or triangles and circles. Majestically, the jukebox sat on casters gripping sturdy oak floors of bars (where dancing was expected), cafes (where an occasional couple might try a little "swing") and of any establishment that would attract people looking for a good time in the good-old days.

Put another nickel in my dad would sing. Surprisingly to us kids, he had sung and played the mandolin in a dance band at the turn of the 19th to the 20th Century in his single days before he married a wonderful Christian lady and settled into family life. *In the nickelodeon, All I want is loving you, And music, music, music.* His singing that song to me gave me a hint of his past. There was a mystery there that was left unsaid and I loved and admired him for it. My so kind and giving mother set the ethical tone for the family with Baptist, Pentecostal, Lutheran and Methodist beliefs all rolled into one and Dad's freethinking ideas thrown into the mix. *Put another nickel in* from my dad was also sung by Teresa Brewer on the nickelodeon.

We need to go way back in the past to 1877, twelve years before both my parents were born in 1889, to find the roots of the jukebox. And what an amazing history it is! In 1877 Thomas Edison discovered how to record speech and thus he invented the phonograph. He recorded sound by engraving waveforms onto a rotating, tinfoil cylinder and it reproduced sound so you could hear what he recorded. As the cylinder rotated, a needle traced the waveforms and vibrated to reproduce the recorded sound waves for listening. After using tin-foil he developed wax cylinders that were used for recording until the round, flat discs that some of us still possess, took over the recording business.

The earliest disc records that played on a phonograph were made, at the end of the 1800s, of various materials, including hard rubber and cellulose. Then a shellac compound, about one-third shellac and two-thirds pulverized rock, known as a "mineral-filler" became standard. The flat disc record was made until the late 1950s and played at a speed of 78 revolutions per minute and is called a "78" by collectors. During and after World War II when shellac supplies were limited, some 78 rpm records were pressed in vinyl instead of shellac, particularly the six-minute 12" 78 rpm records produced by V-Disc for distribution to US troops in World War II. Shortly after the war, in 1948, the '33s' known as 'long play' and the 7 inch '45s' holding one song on each side and called a "single," came along with better sound. From then on the records, made of polyvinyl chloride, were called "vinyl."

So in my youth during the 40s and 50s, the pinnacle years of the jukebox, I probably saw records of all three speeds spinning on that record changer and three-quarters of all records produced went into jukeboxes. Overall a couple million or more jukeboxes graced the planet during its heyday. There are still jukeboxes around using retrofitted old boxes and newer technology like CDs (I'll say no more) and even new jukeboxes made by Rock-ola, the last manufacturer in town after Wurlitzer, AMI and Seeburg left the business long ago.

Going back again to the late 1800s and two years before my parents were born Justus Seeburg left Sweden (my parents forebears' home) in 1887 for America. He started a company making player pianos and other musical devices, including the Audiophone which was an early version of the jukebox. A player piano, which I "played" in my youth, had an electro-mechanical or hand winding mechanism that moved perforated paper rolls inside the piano, which in-turn triggered keys to move and make sound. In the 1890s musical devices that made actual recordings sprang up along with phonograph parlors from New York to Paris. The nickel-in-the-slot phonograph was developed by Glass and Arnold and heard via large, horn-like listening tubes (acoustic headphones). Along came an apparatus that automatically changed records, invented by Hobart C. Niblack in 1918. This led to a "selective" (patron had several choices of recordings) music box as it was called then until the term "jukebox" took hold with the public. Seaborg's' Audiophone had eight separate turntables mounted on a circular, rotating device. Later, his Selectophone could select ten different records mounted vertically on a spindle.

All of these automated, coin-operated musical devices sold well, with continuing improvement of old features and addition of new ones. In the 1930s Justus's son Marshall began focusing exclusively on manufacturing jukeboxes. Early in the 1900s the jukeboxes were called coin-operated phonographs and in the 1930s the word jukebox took over the common usage. The name jukebox probably came from the following bit of history.

The Negro (as the blacks were called in the first half of the 1900s) population in mostly segregated Harlem, south Chicago and throughout the South gathered at seedy roadhouses, dives and low-end bars to have fun and dance. Jook or jouk are the slang words they used meaning "to dance" and "wicked". They created their own dancing or juking called the jitterbug and swing dance that included the Zoot Suit and Lindy hop. They juked to jazz rhythms like bebop and to ragtime and blues music, streaming out of the jook box; music and dances that were unique to the black population and then popularized in the white culture. This juking gave them freedom to wiggle and strut, be uninhibited and silly and most of all fun as in juke. With the African influence the African-Americans danced to the music machine they called a jook box in neighborhood gathering spots, including a juke joint or a roadside dance joint, with maybe a whorehouse and *jouke* meaning "to rest," for an overnight at a southern inn. There were African origins to these "j" words that were used by people who worked in the southern jute fields. Jute, a plant fiber made into gunny sacks for transporting food crops, was grown in Africa and Asia from at least the 16th Century on up to today. The blacks came to America as slaves and worked in the jute fields in the southern states which had an excellent climate for growing jute, until growing cotton surpassed jute. The word "jute" was used in jute joint where people danced to music from the jute box.. Eventually they were called juke joint and jukebox.

There were several important historic events that affected the life of the jukebox. Prohibition from 1920 to 1933 helped secure the jukebox's success. With alcohol banned, people were looking for pleasure and fun and the jukebox provided inexpensive music rather than a costly live band. With the Great Depression, from 1929 to the early 1940s, the jukeboxes' draw was even greater. A jukebox venue provided cheap entertainment. Underground crime was another influence in the jukebox era. The Mafia took hold from at least the 1920s through the 1940s. The government was not very successful is prosecuting their law-breaking and violence. The Mafia dealt in cash and jukeboxes provided them with cash. Organized crime controlled the operation of jukeboxes wherever they could strong-arm the proprietors across the nation, especially in Chicago and New York where they were populous and powerful. The World War II war years, from 1939 to 1945, had a big effect on jukebox popularity. When the war started, production of jukeboxes continued at a slower pace because metal and plastic were needed for the war. But jukebox listening provided entertainment throughout the war years and helped the record industry to sell records since more people were looking for cheap ways to have a good time. Business resumed in an even bigger way when the war ended and the boys came home.

Two of my older four brothers, in the Air Force and the Marine Corps, were in that war and I can tell you there was joy and cause for celebration when the war was won and the surviving soldiers, marines, air force personnel and sailors returned to their hometowns alive, thank the Lord. Music and dance fueled by legal beer and gin with Prohibition being over and done, kept the 1000s of jukeboxes in business during the rest of the '40s and through the '50s and more. Jukeboxes, through those years, showed off variations of styling and colors and showcasing names like Wurlitzer's "Wagon Wheel," "Peacock" and "Colonial," Seeburg's "Classic" and "Envoy," AMI's "Singing Tower" and Rock-Ola's "Spectravox" and "Master Rockolite."

Like everywhere else, bars in my hometown had jukeboxes and dancing, but as a Baptist going to bars was considered sinful, as was dancing, and I wasn't of age anyway and I didn't dance. The jukebox that I knew took up a prominent spot in the City Café and, as a kid and then a teenager, I remember it and also the replacements during the 1940s and the 1950s looking elegant and, with a phrase I learned later, a tribute to Art Deco, a style of rich and vivid colors, strong, symmetrical, geometric shapes and lavish ornamentation. Visual glamour exuded from the surreal box and catchy tunes and touching love songs streamed through the air. It was enough to make you want to laugh or cry and to dance.

Before I leave those days behind, I'll hang out for a while with my two best girl friends at a booth in the City Café (the café is still there but not the jukebox) in the early 1950s and give you a taste of the glory days of the gracefully styled jukebox with a magic glo. The rich sounds of Glen Miller playing *Little Brown Jug* and Elizabeth Cotton singing *Freight Train, freight train, going so fast* came from low output speakers producing low volume, often positioned at the top of the jukebox and covered with grill cloth on the front of the box. The tone-arm held a needle, whose thickness was precisely made to not damage the record and to produce the right amount of sound. As the music faded away, we put a nickel into the slot for one song or a dime to get three songs. The list of titles was lined up in columns along the front with buttons to press for a song. Behind a window of etched glass, the record of our choice swung out on its table and the arm moved over the record with the needle positioned over the outer edge groove leading to the center of the disc. And the music began.

As Time Goes By, written by Herman Hupfeld in 1931, is our pick, made famous in 1942 in the movie "Casablanca." In a popular scene that you may remember, Ilsa (Ingrid Bergman) arrives at Rick's (Humphrey Bogart) Café Americain and asks Sam (Dooley Wilson) to play *As Time Goes By*. Rick and Ilsa had played that song back in Paris when they fell in love. *As Time Goes By* was still around for the three of us and the king of song himself, Frank Sinatra, is crooning. *You must remember this, A kiss is still a kiss, A sigh is still a sigh.* We felt it in our hearts as he continued in his sensuous voice. *The fundamental things apply, As time goes by.* We swayed, we gently moved our arms in slow time, while sitting in our booth, and dreamed on. We had not been kissed. We did not have boyfriends but we wished for it. We could only imagine that sweet kiss with longing. It would happen someday but for today we felt almost a sadness for what we didn't have. *And when two lovers woo, They still say: I love you, On that you can rely.* Oh, how we wanted that for ourselves. *No matter what the future brings, As time goes by.* We girlfriends, braver for being together, could avoid the tears that might have happened alone. Proms that were talked about by our classmates, right there in the café, were out for two of us since Baptists don't dance—or drink or smoke or go to movies, and for all three of us there was the "not feeling included" in the main social circle of our class which pretty much excluded us from the dating scene and being asked to the prom. But our fun and yes, joy, was not deterred. We had the jukebox almost within arms' reach. More tunes would cheer us up and make us hop. We loved them all. We left our empty lime phosphate glasses behind and walked home.

No matter what the future brings Sinatra sang and we didn't know what that future would be. College was on the horizon, we knew that. But the jukebox era of our youth wouldn't ever be the same. Past our college years and almost unbeknownst to us the jukebox started to fade away. People began collecting them as mementos of an irreplaceable time and some were, unimaginable to our sensibilities, destroyed. And a few stuck around in that occasional bar or cafe.

I long for the past, romantic that I am. I wish I could still put another nickel in and hear those tunes again, so firmly etched in our hearts, playing *Swinging On A Star*, *One O'Clock Jump*, *Moonlight Serenade* and yet again, *As Time Goes By*.

So, please, lovers and friends, let's dance one last dance. I stopped being Baptist long, long ago. Any tune you choose is a gift for the senses and we'll go out gently swaying with that gorgeous beacon of colorful light and dreamy sound lighting and steering our way.

And Doris, dear to my heart, *Never thought my heart could be so yearny,* I can hear you singing that last stanza of my journey, through Jukebox time. *Why did I decide to roam? Gotta take that sentimental journey, Sentimental journey home, Sentimental journey!*

Ethel Erickson Radmer

KINDNESS

March 2014

Kindness is a high virtue. It has been put up on a pedestal of attributes we most want in someone. It is a predominant good by any measure of endowments which you or I can possess as well as look for in others to express. And, I'd argue, this bonding and healing trait was noticed, appreciated and sought after way back to the prehistoric people that began to populate our planet. We have quotes from our ancestors' early writings of the importance of kindness that I'll scatter throughout my own writing. But even before those first humans put a marker of some sort to a receptive 'paper' surface to make words, the cavemen of many thousands of years ago painted their cave stone walls and left a pictorial legacy of what was important in their lives. They had intelligence *and* emotion, as researchers have interpreted from the stone-man's colorful and complex drawings. One example is a painting called 'Two Reindeer,' stretched out nine feet wide along the wall of a narrow passage in the cave of Font-de-Gaume in southern France, painted 18,000 years ago. It shows a male caribou reindeer watching over and protecting a female, about to give birth. Artists of all ages capture emotions, moods and feelings in their work and these ancient artists did the same. This cave artist shows a knowing of love and kindness and sets a mood of protection which could be projected on to the animals as well. Animals have emotions as veterinarians will attest to by doing FMRI's showing the same lit-up regions of the brain as humans have and by just being with an animal and its' human companion and seeing the emotional exchange of touching and caring that goes on. Kindness is in all of us! And it has been an innate gift since those first men and women walked the earth. What a beautiful thought. So, what is this sweet gesture loaded with feelings that we call *kindness* and why do we all yearn for it? Let's explore the ins and outs and I'll bring in some personal experience—and we ALL have personal experience!

One time in a discussion group that I was part of a while ago we were all asked by the leader what was the most important quality or ingredient for each of us to have in our daily experience with others. When it came my turn, I answered KINDNESS. After knowing looks of seeming understanding, they wondered why that was my choice. I responded, "It greases the skids. It makes all the happenings in your day move in a smoother more peaceful way. A kindness shown evaporates the tension and lays the bad things to rest. It warms the heart."

And as if to prove the point, during a recent phone conversation I had with an old college friend something came up about people's behavior. I shared with her an emotional hurt that cut sharply long ago and has been repeated in lesser fashion occasionally through the years to renew the hurt and I hadn't been able to rid myself of it totally. As Michael Singer in *the untethered soul* would say, it was a thorn with edges that kept hurting if the right reminder came along.

With utter kindness my friend validated my feelings of hurt in a way that hadn't quite happened before. It was not pejorative, but was understanding of my feelings. The pain passed through my being and the kindness took over and enveloped me. I can still feel it. There was and is no judgment there, no plumbing the exhaustive trials of what all have I done to try to change the situation and to get other people to be more of what I want and think they should try to be. I let it all go and felt the kind warmth of another soul take over and fill the spaces. I felt liberated and that also was a beautiful thing! That's what kindness can do.

And I'll add now, kindness works in more than one direction. It is wonderful to receive and it makes a difference in so many ways and it is extraordinary to give. Being kind to someone makes you yourself feel good. It warms your own heart. To see or imagine someone's response to your gesture of kindness is a pleasure. Goodness rebirths goodness. I did this well over a dozen years ago, before 'acts of kindness' caught the media's attention and became contagious. Crossing the Golden Gate Bridge from Marin to San Francisco, I paid my bridge toll, I think four dollars at the time, and spontaneously also paid for the car behind me. I watched in my rearview mirror and imagined the driver surprised and pleased when he passed through. It was just plain fun. Another year someone did the same for me and I rejoiced again.

A host of words and phrases describe kindness: a benevolent turn, showing compassion, a tender quality, a helpful deed, a friendly feeling, generous, a kind act and loving. The word kind means humane, as in compassion shown to others of the animal kingdom and to ourselves. You are kindhearted if you show a desire to promote the welfare or happiness of others. It is all to the good.

By way of their paintings, the cave dwellers of centuries ago were shown to give reverence to nature, as later on along history's timeline, the American Indians, with awe and wonder, gave spiritual meaning to the natural world. And kindness was in their being. The gorgeous, sensitive renderings of curves of the deer manifest that. And when many organized forms of religion and worship did take hold on up to the present they make a good case for kindness. Kindness fills the pages.

Throughout the Old Testament books of Genesis, Joshua and Ruth, through the Proverbs to Jeremiah and Jonah, kindness is shown, requested, appreciated, hoped for and given freely. King Solomon of Israel and son of David wrote (King James Version) in Psalms 119:76 "Let, I pray thee, thy merciful kindness be for my comfort, according to thy word unto thy servant." Isaiah 54:10 "For the mountains shall depart, and the hills be removed; but my kindness shall not depart from thee ... saith the Lord." And in the New Testament we have Paul (Saul) of Tarsus writing the Ephesians in chapter 4, verse 32, "And be ye kind one to another, tenderhearted, forgiving one another, even as God for Christ's sake hath forgiven you" and Simon Peter saying in II Peter 1:7, "And (add) to godliness brotherly kindness; and to brotherly kindness charity."

Kindness and charity go hand in hand. Translation of the Bible into English goes back to Latin and to the Greek where the Greek words *chrestotes* for kindness and *agape* for loving-kindness and to the Latin *caritas* for charity come together. And the Bible is filled with references to charity, with probably the best known in I Corinthians 13:13: "And now abideth faith, hope, charity, these three; but the greatest of these (is) charity." Both charity and kindness are doing and being good to others. God holds them in high esteem.

The Quran speaks of the prophet Muhammad as "gentle and kind" and teaching kindness and compassion and, in Chapter and Verse 17:23 and in 4:36, Allah instructs the Muslims to be kind to your parents, kin, neighbors, orphans, the destitute and to your soul. We in this modern age need to be reminded of that last one! The translators saw that your 'self' and your soul were like one and the same. So be kind to yourself and you are being kind to your soul.

Philosophers and deep thinkers through the ages have explored and extolled kindness. Confucius (551 BC - 479 BC) gave us five things to practice in life: courtesy, generosity, honesty, persistence and kindness. Kindness is in good company! Confucius also admonished us to "never forget kindnesses." Compassion, a close relative of kindness, was a fundamental ethical incentive in Arthur Schopenhauer's (1788-1860) philosophical school of thought. He said that we are motivated to seek the well-being of others and alleviate their woes. Friedrich Nietzsche (1844-1900) proposed that kindness and love are the "most curative herbs and agents in human intercourse." Albert Einstein (1879–1955) said that kindness, beauty and truth were the ideals that lighted his way. Those timeless beacons (my phrase) continually gave him courage to be cheerful about life.

Now, it's a reality of life that kindness does not always prevail, as much as we feast on it and freely give it away. And, at the same time, we may be filled with it almost every waking moment for our entire lives—it IS possible! Witness the Dalai Lama who says, "There is no need for temples; no need for complicated philosophy. Our own brain, our own heart is our temple; the philosophy is kindness." Kindness permeates his words and infuses his actions. In all his writings (I've read stacks of his books) and articles about his dealings with warmongers, his traveling the world for gatherings and conferences of all sorts (I've been to two, one of which was 'up close and personal' enough to hear every chuckle and see every line of his face in a smile) this man radiates kindness. Jesus was presented in a similar 'kindness persona' by the prophets whose writings fill the New Testament. Jesus forgave people their wrongdoings. He blessed the multitudes, performed miracles of health and providing food and he gave freely of his love and kind actions.

That sounds all well and good. But the rest of the world may not be enhancing the feel-good endorphins. As I see it, there are three areas that are especially prone to unkindness. And this is worth exploring for 'kindness sake!' Two groups, the business world and the political engines running our countries, are especially vulnerable to indifference and harshness. Their bigness is a part of the problem—big is not better! Business can be hardnosed and rough and people are not always treated well in the workplace. But you can make it fun and life-enhancing and at the same time produce a terrific product or service. I see good signs in business to humanize and harmonize their relations with the public and with their employees—its good business to do that!

On the political scene, governments around the globe need steady monitoring of abuses to our identity and validation of our freedom to choose in almost any area of our lives. In our own government for the good of yes—KINDNESS, what I see is 'the less government the better.' The money that goes into government programs is misused and wasted and feeds an entitlement mentality among its benefactors. Accepting yourself as victim and feeling others owe you something is not kind to yourself or others! Taxpayers that want those programs for others are 'getting themselves off the hook' and abdicating their own goodness to give and thinking "it's off my conscience" because the government is taking care of it, rather than personally, through small private and religious projects, addressing needs hands-on and directly and not multi-layered and huge like government programs are. "The government does not do well at being kind," you can quote me. And to quote my friend Nietzsche again, he didn't like government either. In his 1881 book (yes, I've read several of his heavy books), *The Dawn of Day*, # 179, he said "AS LITTLE STATE AS POSSIBLE!" And "it would be better to let the machinery (of this 'workshop' which is the government) work itself to pieces again! ... however much it may babble about economy, is a spendthrift: it wastes intellect, the most precious thing of all." He had a lot more to say about what is wrong with government, but you have the idea! Let's pass on kindness from our own hands and hearts and not expect someone or something else to do it for us. We're getting out of the habit of extending kindness and of people working harder at meeting their own needs. Kindness and freedom go hand-in-hand. No one forces you to be kind. Kindness is a gift. Be free as the wild horses of yore stampeding on Ocracoke, with a hitch: to be kind to the other for your own kind's sake.

The third zone of unkindness, that I see, is in our social discourse. Both the media and fast-changing technology let loose a torrent of bad manners to say the least and of more extreme base, hurtful and sharp exchanges that are bruising our souls and psyches and have even led to suicide. Bullying is not funny. Laughing should be good for you. Comedians on the 'tube' have a big influence with their huge audience of followers, generally of the same political persuasion as the comedian and a lot of humor is political humor. So the comic's humor is mostly about people they don't like or agree with and if you, the listener, agree with that you laugh. Making fun of people and things is their modus operandi. Again, as I see it, pop culture as reflected in the comedic world's playbook—and it is funny whatever your political persuasion if you have a sense of humor—is pretty much locked up by the political left. Check out the stand-up comics for yourself! Making people a joke works as long as we have the good humor to make fun of ourselves. Someone or something has to be the butt of their barbs. We can survive the hits and have the openness to laugh out loud or 'lol,' using one of the abbreviations of phrases of our modern, fast-paced way to communicate. Sharp humor seems to be part of the game. But how do we reconcile the biting and mocking that goes on in a comedic routine with being kind? It's a stretch but let's look at the jibes as yet another talent and skill along the breadth of human possibility. And even if they're roasting you or your kind, laugh at the humor of it. We can accept that it's happening and play the game, but not let it become the rational, non-comedic discourse of our daily lives. In the midst of this we can elevate our lives by treating others and ourselves kindly.

What more can we do? Rise above it, I say. Be the kind of person you want to see in others. Know that people are not perfect. Buck the trend with your own grace, just as the Tibetan monks tortured by the Chinese invaders, feel loving-kindness in the face of the hater and mocker. The haters can't hurt you emotionally if you don't let them. Your deflector is your shield of good-will and a warm heart. Kindness wins and sometimes wins over the unsuspecting. This balm of kindness is like the African American spiritual I loved to sing in my school days and the tenderness of it would bring me to tears. "There is a balm in Gilead, To make the wounded whole." Kindness is the balm and it works both ways: yours to me and mine to you. Revel in the joy of it! And let it touch your soul.

To add to your own bottomless reservoir of gestures of kindness (we all have it if only we think to access it!) try these that have worked for me. Tell a former teacher what an impact they had on your life. Do it before it's too late! I did it the summer of 2013, with a visit to my high school science and math teacher, and it was touching and so sweet. I praised him and he turned it around again and again to praise me! That is what kindness does! What a teacher he was and what a gift he gave me and continued to give by giving me kindness in return.

Bring your unused blankets, coats, shoes and household items cluttering your shelves and filling up a space to a charity (that's not a bad word!) shop or a homeless shelter. I do it frequently—and shop at the same time in their for-resale store for old items you can't find anymore.

Let someone go ahead of you in line. And then, really engage the eyes of the cashier or ticket taker with a smile on your face and a kind word and keep it up.

If someone is rude to you, don't be angry or edgy in return, but be patient and understanding—even to say, "I'm sorry I cut you off" or "If I was unkind, please forgive me" with a warm smile. If we can manage that, you can feel their anger melt away.

Give your books away. I've given thousands of my books to others when I am done with them and if I need one of them again for my writing or a reread, I buy another or request it from the public library. Or I buy a bunch of an especially good book and pass them on to whomever I think might like it.

Surprise your loved ones by ordering a pizza (knowing what their tastes are), pizza-van delivered to their door, if their life is frazzled or order a flower arrangement delivery if they're going through hard times. I've done it and it is a warm massage to both our hearts.

Write letters and greeting cards to people you love because that doesn't happen a lot these days. It's a treat to find something good in your mailbox.

Complement people sincerely for what you see as good. Say "thank you!" out loud for anything you appreciate and that includes "Welcome!" to the baby turtles just hatched in your small lake and "thank you" to the trees for filling the woods and to the creator of each good thing. Frederic Delarue, an author and musician, wraps his long arms around a tree and talks softly to ask its permission to take a leaf or a piece of fruit. I've been in his presence and I can tell you that kindness fills his being.

Take time to be a good listener to someone in distress. Don't judge or pity or dominate with suggestions but show understanding and kindness. Do this often and it becomes part of your being. And the stranger or loved one might pass on the good will and return the kindness to someone else. A dark day could become a bright day. A dejected soul might be transformed. Happiness and self-worth would be on the rise. Let's all be kind and we will change the world.

Ethel Erickson Radmer

LOOK and LISTEN

October 2014

The eyes and ears are such powerful senses. They dominate our experiences in life, as seen reflected in literature, art, the essentials of living such as getting and consuming food and water, our avocations and earning our way, mixing in society and as heard in music, nature's sounds and in our talking with each other. We have a golden chance in this brief life to realize the beauty, color and gift of perceiving an amazing world with our eyes and ears.

Our eyes are cameras, collecting and sending images of our surroundings to our brains to perceive. Our ears catch the waves of sound through the mediums of air, water and solid, pass them along to the brain faster than a supercomputer, and register the waves as music, voice, animal growls and barks and as a babbling brook. What we can do with it is to take it in and fully experience this moment and the next moment as it comes and the next and to be fully awake, present and aware of what is happening now, touching to the depths of who we are. And listen also, to the silence, as on the moon and look at the beauty of a lost loved one in your mind's eye.

What we see and hear is guided first by our physical and neuronal capacity to get messages and to comprehend their meaning and second by our own array of beliefs and system of values. We look and listen through the filter of things we think are so, the variety of which makes for a rich tapestry of voices from many points of view.

To get a sense of the labyrinth of possibilities of observation I asked five people if they would look and listen for an hour and see and note whatever came up for them, to keep as focused in the present moment as they could be on 'look and listen,' in whatever setting they chose, and to write down their impressions. Two people were male and three were female. Their age range was from 17 years to 87 years, with a wide variety of beliefs and situations in life. I'm using their first names and I had space for some but not all of their writing, with my comments here and there. The excursion of Jeff, 59 years old, in Indiana, will start us off and appear throughout the essay. This is look and listen, transcribed from audiotape, through Jeff's eyes and ears.

So today we're going to go on a walk in the woods. Before we even get to the woods on the road in, we'll stop and listen and off to the left is a brown thrasher. The brown thrasher is a bird that has a distinctive call. Like a mocking bird it has a huge variety of sounds that it makes; unlike a mocking bird it usually makes its calls in pairs. And looking around, a butterfly flies by. A great blue heron sails by overhead and there's the buzz of an airplane, a small propeller job, crossing the sky nearby. To one side of the road is a stream. There's the sound of water falling over the rocks. Most of those sounds are all the birds and different kinds of birds calling. I'm on a gravel road now walking into the place where I entered the woods. I like to walk in the areas where the gravel is not so thick because that's quieter. One thing about walking in the woods that I learned long ago, as a boy, is that you have to be very quiet, because usually if you're going to find a creature in the woods, you'll hear it and you'll see it. If you're making too much noise clomping around then you can't hear anything but your own clomping around. You have a much better chance of seeing the animals that live here, not disturbing them. And if you find a spot and sit quietly, usually for fifteen minutes to half an hour, they'll get busy again and they don't really notice you. It's spring, early May here. The May apples have leafed out. The ferns have greened up and have leaves. A lot of the trees, they're just starting to leaf out, very light green leaves mostly.

The early spring is Morel season and people around here seem to get really excited about that. I haven't had much luck finding them myself, but I keep going out and looking. Morels are quite nice but my favorite is hen-of-the-woods, also called maitaki or in Japan, the king of mushrooms, but they don't come out until October. Finding Morels is all about looking, since mushrooms don't make noise (chuckle on audio tape). They just sit there. They do have a distinctive appearance which makes them easy to find, well not easy to find, because they are very well camouflaged. They sort of resemble pine cones, but they tend to grow in underbrush and places where you have to sort of root around to find them (crunching leaves and twittering birds).

You have to kick where you place your feet carefully, avoiding reeds and sticks and branches and leaves as much as possible. Just transfer your weight gradually and stop ever so often and just listen. Birds. There's a jet flying by overhead. A few minutes ago I could hear a pair of geese honking their way through the sky. The breeze is pretty gentle right now, so it's not making much noise, but you can feel it, coolness on your skin. The sun is warm and filtering through the new leaves. That's the sound of small insects buzzing by, probably flies, wild violets on the forest floor. A bumble bee's buzzing by. A centipede has two little antennae on its head that are very active, seems to be hearing everything in front of it. Still in the vicinity of the creek a little frog just jumped in from the shore and swam under a rock to hide from me.

Oh, hello. Hmm. So there are box turtles here in the woods. I just met one that's right at the edge of the creek. Almost stepped on the poor guy, he pulled his head back a little bit and that motion is how I noticed. Oh, looks like an older box turtle. The shell is dark brown and yellow. He's pulling back a little bit because I'm talking too loud and it's not to his liking or her liking, I can't tell. So I walk around and let the box turtle be on his or her way (creek water bubbling over rock).

Nature is a treasure trove of sights and sounds to fill the senses but Alissa, age 47, in North Carolina, chose to look inside and listen to her inner voice.

It is time to look inward and to listen to your heart.

It is time to review your reality and to face your deepest fears, to bring them to the light of consciousness, to acknowledge them, and to transmute them in order to welcome in a new era of peace.

Steve Beckow defines a "core issue" as an issue you hide from others or even yourself that you would rather die than face. Your core issues have a huge impact on your words, actions and deeds. They influence how you are creating your reality and the amount of joy you allow into your life. Whether from childhood or a past life, core issues run deep beneath the surface yet constantly sprout throughout your life and your creations.

It is time to look beneath the surface of your reality and face these deep obstructions. This journey takes quiet introspection and courage. Listen to your heart in quiet meditation. Listen to your inner child as well as those around you (your family, your closest friends). Ask Spirit to show you what you need to know ... and then listen. With calm detachment, learn what your core issues are and look at how they emerge through you.

You may not like what you hear and see but when you recognize your core issues and face them with courage through acknowledgement and reflection, you shine a light on those shadows and they will dissolve as shadows do. You transmute them with light and with your intention to process and to heal them. Then you can move forward into a new state of being.

Kaypacha says the coming full moon is a time of great illumination. The entire Universe is blocking us from distractions and forcing us to look inward and, hopefully, to listen to our hearts. Now is the time to summon the courage to enact this deep healing.

Look and listen and move forward. A peaceful planet awaits.

Even with a lessening or a total absence of the senses of sight and sound, you can examine your inner being, as Alissa shows. And from my own experience, looking inward can make for an enriched life beyond what you might imagine.

With senses intact, Sachin, a seventeen year-old senior in high school, saw the natural and material world around him, examined what was important to him and expressed his concerns and what we might do about it. He wrote it in a poem.

Look and Listen
Look at the world passing by
Smile as time flies past your eyes
Listen to your voice
Now make a choice
You can be heard
Not just by anyone but by a bird
Life is dying all around
Only humans don't fall down
We have to do something for nature

For our world's dying creatures
We can no longer listen to the cries of nature
For we only talk about change in lectures
We don't look to make a change
But we want to, isn't that strange?
We listen to family and friends
But soon our world will end
We will all die one day
That is why I just want to say
We can turn this around; we can make a fight
There is still hope with sunlight
We can get rid of harmful pollution
And smile at a new solution
Listen for the pleas of our planet
Look for a way that we can change it

My 86 year old cousin, Eunice, pure of heart, has lived on a farm in Wisconsin all of her life and she continues to live by her Christian beliefs. Still canning the summer garden produce, staying healthy, sweet and kind, and wanting others to be saved, she wrote this:

As human beings we have been endowed by our creator with five great senses—namely sight, hearing, touch, taste and smell. We are particularly speaking about two of the senses which may mean the most to us—the sense of sight and the sense of sound or hearing. If we were blind we could not look into the faces of our dear loved ones. Nor see the pretty flowers and trees, and the beautiful landscapes. We would not be able to enjoy ourselves in reading a book or see a child snuggling up with one of his favorite pets—a puppy or a little kitten or the one who picked a beautiful little bouquet of wildflowers to give to some loved one.

If we could not hear we would not be able to listen to the voices of our loved ones—to hear the cry of a child or someone in distress or the happy sound of children at play or receiving of a gift. We would not hear the beautiful sounds of birds, such as the meadowlarks, the robins, the chickadees, and the interesting call of the whip-poor off in the distant forest. We would not be able to hear the breezes among the trees nor the rippling of the waters in the brooks and on the river. We would not be able to listen to the beautiful songs and hymns of the church and all the musical instruments and organs that may accompany them.

However even though some have gone through one or more of these difficulties, there are those, who have by faith, risen to great accomplishments, trying to do what they could in life. Fanny Crosby is a good example. She was born in Southwestern New York in 1820 and passed away in 1915, but became blind when she was only six weeks old. She was educated at the New York Institution for the Blind, where she was encouraged to write poetry. She began writing hymns in 1864 to a total of more than 6000 hymns. Among the most famous of these are " Safe in the Arms of Jesus," Rescue the Perishing," "Pass me Not," and "Blessed Assurance." She looked to God for her help and listened to Him as He brought Spiritual truths to her mind. She became a great blessing to the world.

We look into a mirror. We want to see how we look. Do we like what we see? If we do not—we listen to the feelings of our heart and try to change. Maybe we would like to change the style of our hair. James, Chapter one in the Bible, speaks about those who hear the Word of God and don't do what it says. They are like a man beholding himself in a glass, (mirror). He looks at himself and goes his way, forgetting what manner of man he was. However, if he would listen to the Word of God and do what it says, he would be blessed.

The human heart is looking for something that will satisfy. We long for peace and happiness, but some people are looking to things that will not satisfy such as wealth, fame, and fortune. Some look to worldly pleasures to help them to feel good. Some indulge in drugs and other things that lead down the wrong path. Many become discouraged and give up in despair. Hopelessness fills their hearts.

God has the answer. In the King James Version of the Bible in Isaiah 45:22 it says: "Look unto me and be ye saved, all the ends of the earth; for I am God, and there is none else."

Years ago when I was attending North Central Bible Institute (now called North Central University) in Minneapolis, Minnesota, there was a large sign up above the downtown area of the city that was put up by the Christian Businessmen. It said "Have You Ever Wondered Is Real Lasting Peace Possible? Christ is the Answer." Psalm 121:1,2 says: "I will lift up mine eyes unto the hills, from whence cometh my help. My help cometh from the Lord, which made heaven and earth."

Holding onto her religious dogma of the past and always living her present life for the future of redemption and paradise serves Eunice well in living a productive, thankful and joy filled life. The present, the now, the moment we are in, followed by another moment is for her not the be all and end all of her existence. Heaven is in her future. And look and listen are winding through her time on earth like a web.

Letting go, now, of the analogies and figures of speech in Eunice's religious world, we return to Jeff who continues on the trail in the 'touch it—it's real' world of nature.

I just disturbed a squirrel and it has scampered away along a fallen log with its tail raised high and climbed up a tree and it's up there chattering at me to let me know that it thinks I don't belong here, Or maybe it's just letting the other squirrels know that there's something around that they should be aware of, mainly me. Thank goodness the mosquitoes aren't out in force yet, It's a lot more pleasant without them constantly buzzing you.

There is logging in this area. The loggers just take a few trees. A surprising number of trees, all due to natural forces, there's one across from me, a very large oak, split right down the middle, lightning strike that blew the whole of the bark off all around the tree. It's kind of astonishing how much power there was in that lightning to do that much damage. They do get some strong winds through here. As the big trees come down, some of the smaller trees also get hit.

Sitting still for a moment and focusing on the very small, it's just amazing how much activity there is in every little part of the forest floor. The ants of several types scurrying across the leaves, other insects going about their business, the mosses growing on the fallen branches and it's too small to see like the microorganisms. the worms under the ground, the creatures that live in holes, the logs and under the logs, the bugs, spiders in their webs, the flies of course, small plants, grasses, shrubs, every little part of the forest is alive.

(crunchy steps) This is not an example of walking quietly (chuckle). I'm pretty noisy. The wind is starting to pick up and I can hear it moving through the leaves at the top of the trees as a puff, as the sailors like to call it, approaches and the word for that sound from one of my favorite authors, Terry Pratchett for his susurrus. Look in the direction of the sound. You can see the leaves and the branches in the treetops moving more actively as the sound approaches and the poplar tree sways back and forth (birds are twittering).

The perceptions of someone with late stage Lewy Body Dementia (related to Alzheimer's) are unknown because so little is expressed, except an occasional person on their death-bed suddenly speaking clearly and coherently, to the mourners around her. Ruth had dementia about 7-8 years from early signs, to late stage. What follows gives an idea of how she viewed her world with the encouragement and recording by her daughter. Though little was said by Ruth, I have always felt there is a lot more going on in the consciousness of people with Dementia and Alzheimer's than shows in their language.

The nursing supervisor at the Four Winds Manor in Verona WI, said to say the phrase "Look and Listen" more simply, just say one word, "Look", and after a while "Listen". He said people with later stages of dementia, have trouble with multi step directions, so the simpler the better. As we proceeded, it didn't make a big difference. I said "Look" and then a prompt later, I said "Listen" and a prompt later, I also used the phrase "Look and Listen".

Claire, who is four years old, and I went to visit my mom, Ruth, Tuesday morning for an hour. She was in a wheel chair in the aviary room with a nice seating area when we arrived.

I said hello to my mom. She said, "Hi". She was looking at a newspaper when I came in. I sat down right next to her so I could hear her. She talks softly and can mumble her words sometimes. I began by saying "Look", then a pause when no response, I said "what do you hear?" She looks at the newspaper. She looks at Claire. She then looked at the birds and said, "Oh, look at the birds!" (Aviary where the beautiful finches are flying around, some making a nest). She then looks around, looks at people walking through, the birds and Claire coloring on the carpet, and smiles when looking at Claire. She then says, "She cried according to..." She then looks up and smiles again and says hi to the administrator when the person walks by and goes into the office and says, "Hello Ruth." My mom also laughs a little bit and she sees another person dressed in office wear and Mom says, "Businesslike."

I said "Listen," and waited a long time, it does take a while for a response. When I don't get one I ask, "What do you hear?" She says, "Hmmmm" and shrugs. She then says, "I'll think about it awhile." After a while she says, "A hundred and eighty dollars." When looking at Claire coloring a picture of a farm scene, I say "Listen" again. She looks at the paper and says, "Can I take a look?" and laughs. She looks at the various sounds she hears, the bird, people talking, Claire coloring, the wheels of a cart going by...

Someone walks by and says, hi. She pauses and says, "Hi." And she smiles. When I say "Look" "Listen," or "Look and Listen" she tries to say something, but she can't. She forgets what she is trying to say. She looks at Claire coloring her picture and Mom says, "On top of the hill," (There is a house on a hill in the picture). She then mumbles and looks around. She brushes the crumbs off her lap.

A maintenance worker walks by in the hallway. Mom says, "He looks familiar." I say "Look." She says, "A lot of crayons, colors." She looks to the birds. She looks toward where the maintenance men are talking. She looks toward where the TV is located, and at Claire coloring. She looks at the administrator dressed up in a longish wool skirt, button down shirt and wool blazer, and says, "She looks like a teacher." That is true. She did really look like she could have been a teacher (an old fashioned one). She then asks, "Is it 4:00?" Claire then finishes her picture. Mom says, "She's got that." She then looks at the phone when it is ringing. I say "Look" again and she says "Look at the birds flying." A motorized wheelchair goes by making a squeaking sound. She looks towards the wheelchair. She then said "I have to purchase a peach." Then we had to leave to get Claire off to 4K. We said our goodbyes and she waved to me.

Ruth died about five months after this conversation. Near death she did have what is called *terminal lucidity,* a lucid moment when cognition, memory and insight are present. She was aware of everything around her. She tried to communicate, but couldn't really speak at the end. Her daughter thinks she heard everything they were saying, maybe understood too. It seemed like she did in her reactions, and facial expressions she was trying to make.

Jeff continued sharing his experience to the end of his walk:

The underbrush can be kind of thick and you have to pick a path through the underbrush. A lot of times it won't be a clear path. You have to move branches out of the way or just push through them. The birds are so noisy here it's almost like being in a crowd where you stop listening to them but they're chattering away. These large woodpeckers here are pileated woodpeckers, a relative of the largest woodpecker in the country, the Ivory Bill, which is now believed to be extinct. Pileateds are fairly common here. They're not all that shy. They do (chuckle) very loud drumming sounds. I guess it's part of the territorial display. I'm going to go in this thicket because wild mushrooms seem to like thickets for some reason. But, nothing here today, except a few May apples, and leaves and trillion and beautiful mosses and ferns and many things but not any mushrooms. I'm going to visit with one of the best landmarks in this part of the woods. It's a very old tree, it's a beech tree. It's been here quite a while it seems. It's on a very narrow ridge. It's gripping the ridge on both sides as the ground drops away rapidly. The roots turn into the support braces as they merge with this enormous trunk. The bark is split in places. It's lost some big branches in recent years. Still here, still living and doing well. This particular spot is a spot I come in July because it's covered with Tantarell Mushrooms. Ah. There are no trails leading here. Just have to know where it is. Learning your way in the woods is not much different than learning your way in a neighborhood. Learn the major landmarks and thoroughfares like the ridges and the streams, start exploring locally and then as you learn the landmarks expand outwards till you can go far and wide and know where you are without trails and without a compass and without GPS. If you don't know what time it is you can tell what direction north, south, east and west are just from the sun. Can you tell I used to be a boy scout? Truly I've always liked spending time in the woods. I do it a lot. And the woods themselves are your teacher. In an area now where there are freesias white blossoms all around, those really fine sights of springtime here. That's about it for today. I'm going to find my way back out. Hope you've enjoyed this walk in the woods.

I am grateful for my senses (and to the writers!). To look through my eyes as a babe was to take in a big, new world of color, shapes, dimensions and movement. To hear with my ears the sounds of people talking to me, laughing, singing and the piano playing, to hear my own sounds of cooing and crying and to start to discern the sounds of nature, all surprising and wondrous vibrations in my ears and body, was a joy without bounds. And it continues now in this moment and will in the next and the next. Look and listen.

Ethel Erickson Radmer

MOON

September 2013 with an October 2014 update

Did you know that the moon is drifting farther and farther away from the earth? That is what physicists tell us and they're not too often wrong. By their calculations, every year the moon moves 4 centimeters further away from us than it already is, at 250,000 miles distance. Four centimeters is 1.5748 inches and that might not seem like much, but it adds up over centuries and eons of time. It's a trend worth noting.

Why is it moving away, you wonder, when we all thought it was a love affair, earth with the moon that would last forever? Physicists like Brian Cox and Jeff Forshaw, authors of *why does E=mc2?,* say it is to conserve angular momentum. For a non-physicist like myself, that is a little hard to understand, but I'll make a stab at explaining. Here are my bullets of what I learned from my reading to give the picture of what is happening.

- The moon pulls on our ocean (tidal friction)
- The earth's rate of spin (rotation) slows down.
- Our day lengthens
- The angular (rotational) momentum (mass x distance x velocity) reduces over time.
- This angular momentum that we are losing by tidal friction is transferred to the moon.

- The moon speeds up in its orbit around the earth to compensate for the earth's slowing down its own rotation.
- The moon drifts farther away from the earth into a wider orbit.
- It is happening right now to ensure that the angular momentum of the earth and the moon is conserved to compensate for the earth's rate of spin slowing down, which must happen by the laws of physics.

Whether or not the 'why' makes sense to us, it is a little alarming. The thought of our anchor in the sky, our partner whom we assumed would always and forever be faithful in sharing our space together, shatters our illusions. In spite of modern science liking invariance in order to uncover the universal, change is in the air or space or dark matter, whatever the scientists will settle on calling it. That rocky ball of moon dust is making a long distance move. Granted a noticeable change won't be in our lifetime and maybe not in a huge number of generations. But there is still a sense of loss in knowing the moon is moving on.

We have such a stake in the moon. Not to mention the astronauts—fly me to the moon, who put a solid stake there, saying we were here, and leaving their footprints and rovers behind in the rocky dust. We all had a part in sending our human life over there in a spaceship, launched by a rocket, funded by our government (that be us) and driven by our wanting to know if there is life out there. Several Apollo missions, from 1969 to 1972, brought back 842 pounds of lunar rock and soil. Some of the bounty was loaned out, some lost or stolen, some put on display and some is still being studied while stored in nitrogen (no moisture). Their age was measured by radiometric dating as from 3.16 billion years to 4.5 billion years old, the latter being the same age of our big rock of a moon and of the earth. Conclusions were that the samples from the pockmarked moon surface and just below contained no water. But water was identified in the plume of material thrown up from the surface of the moon by the impact of the lunar module, The samples of rock and soil gave no evidence of living organisms at any time in the Moon's history. Not even once in a blue moon.

Well, that answers that, I guess. No life discovered, but they uncovered, for what it's worth, a treasure trove of titanium that is light weight, very strong and corrosion resistant. It is found on the moon and on the earth in volcanic rock called basalts, with some lunar rocks holding ten times as much titanium as do rocks on Earth. Titanium is abundant on the Moon! This valuable element Ti is used as an alloy in aerospace, buildings, cars, electric power plants, sporting goods and a lot more. If we ever run out we can mine the moon and call ourselves moonrakers. But be aware that gravity's pull is much less on the moon than on Earth, about one-sixth of ours, and that could ease the heavy lifting. You jump one foot on earth for a leap of six feet on the Moon. And, for the record, there is no air as well as no water and thus there is no sound on the moon. Sound needs a medium to carry it, be it air, water or solid.

Moonlight is really sunlight reflected from the surface of the Moon so we can see color. The landscape surface of the Moon is colored light gray and is nearly devoid of strong colors. In the day, from Earth, it can appear white, and at night have a yellow tint, or show a darker yellow to orange in the autumn. The temperature on the Moon varies greatly, from 253 Fahrenheit during the day on the sunlit side to -387 Fahrenheit at night, the dark side that we never see, because of no atmosphere to block the Sun's rays or to trap heat at night. There is no oxygen on the Moon, but other gases like neon, helium, hydrogen, methane, carbon dioxide and ammonia have been discovered in the very thin lunar atmosphere. Sodium and potassium were also found. It all adds up to a place that is not hospitable for human life but a great place to visit and learn and maybe still uncover life or remnants of life hiding deep down to the core. Moon colonies, mini-dwellings, to house humans, that control temperature and provide life-sustaining oxygen, water and food and are sealed off from the harsh environment of the moon, are a distant fancy. Like the old expression 'man in the moon' meant a mythical character who lives in or on the moon but it is an unlikely reality—a little 'moony' in fact.

Where did the moon come from? Perhaps a chunk of earth broke off and started circling the Earth. Or it may have been a wandering body that formed elsewhere in the solar system, such as a moon of Venus that got away, and was captured by Earth's gravity as it passed close by. Another explanation is in traces that may have been found in moon rock, of a possible planet called Theia that is theorized to have collided with Earth when the Earth and Moon were born 4.5 billion years ago. Theira was a goddess in Greek mythology, the mother of Selene who was goddess of the Moon.

Which moves us back to centuries ago when early humans, especially then, were 'over the moon' in their fascination and vital interest in the big ball in the sky. How far back can we go? If we predate recorded history or prehistoric ages to the time Homo sapiens developed, we have a range of time from 200,000 BC to 35,000 BC. If we add the years leading to 2,000 BC, we are then including the Stone Age, Bronze Age and Iron Age. Written historic records in prehistoric times do not exist that we know of, but stunning art did exist on cave walls and in stone formations and ancient artifacts. And the moon is present and prominent in the artist's creations.

Cavemen lived in 28,000 BC and they filled their stone walls with art to include the Moon. In 13,000 BC those prehistoric humans made paintings of groups of dots and squares among bulls, antelope and horses, depicting the 29-day cycle of the Moon. They survived on cave walls in Lascaux, France and were interpreted by Dr. Michael Rappenglueck of the University of Munich. A series of dots curving away from the main row of dots shows the time of the new Moon when it disappears from the sky for several days.

In 6,000 BC the Egyptians, who had their own Moon gods, Osiris and Krons, and the Middle Easterners and North Africans all knew the phases of the moon, the changing of seasons and eclipses, and showed it in their drawings and paintings on stone. They drew lunar calendars and made clocks to help them plan for growing of crops, hunting of animals and religious events. They saw that the moon revolved around the earth in a 29-day cycle. They worshipped the Sun but watched the Moon with fear and awe as it disappeared in eclipses and then reappeared.

Broadly between 3100 BC and 2400 BC, Stonehenge, on a plain just north of what is now Salisbury, England, was built. From an arrangement and moving around of huge stones, ancient worshippers could calculate positions of the sun and moon and phases and cycles of the moon, even predicting a 56-year cycle of moon eclipses. I saw Stonehenge twice in 2001, the sky filmed with a light gray haze, no sun or moon to be seen, but the circle of stones stood out like the ancient monolith it is.

The Bible and other religious texts are part of our early recorded history. The Old Testament, 1400 BC to 400 BC, way before Jesus' day in the years between 1 BC and 1 AD, has Psalm 104:19 (KJV) saying, "He appointed the moon for seasons" and Psalms 8:3, "When I consider thy heavens, the work of thy fingers, the moon and the stars, which thou hast ordained; What is man, that thou are mindful of him?" In Sanskrit and Hindi, Chandra is the god of the moon. And he is one of dozens of Moon gods and goddesses in other cultures. Somewhere between 600 BC and 300 BC (ancient dates are often in disagreement or controversial), Lao-tzu founded

Taoism, a Chinese spiritual tradition and wrote a small book, The Tao Te King. In it he spoke philosophically of the finger pointing to the moon. The finger is the pointer to the moon's location, but the finger is not the moon. As the laughing Chinese Buddha Hotei does in a painting circa 900 AD, you look beyond your finger to gaze at the moon. Take the moon for what it is, he is saying, it is a mystery and not of our making.

Leaving BC and all the dwellers in pre and early history behind, we make a turn into the Dark and Middle Ages (0 - 1500 AD), on up to the Industrial Age ending in 1900 AD, to the Modern or Atomic Age (1900 AD to our present day), all of us continuing to gaze at the moon, learning more and more and yearning to step foot on the Moon and see it up close and personal.

Astronomy is one of the oldest sciences and prehistoric cultures left artifacts like the Egyptian pyramids, brimming with mathematical implications, reaching to the sky. And many other civilizations, including the Greek, Chinese, Indians, Maya, Iranian and Babylonian, had their own ways of observing the sky. Astronomy progressed in 200 AD from Ptolemy's mathematical system of the Earth lying immobile at the center of the rotating universe to more informed and advanced thinking throughout the centuries. Copernicus' (1473-1543) heliocentric model of the Solar System came along, making the sun the center of the universe with the planets orbiting around it, which dealt a blow to the Earth-centric system of Ptolemaic.

At the turn of the 1500s to the 1600s, the telescope was invented and it was a huge advance for viewing the heavens, moon included, and for understanding our place in it. Galileo Galilei (1564-1642) heard about glass lenses being made and he used the idea to make his own telescope. Most scientists at the time believed that all the heavenly bodies including the Moon were perfectly round and smooth. Galileo found that was not true. He saw a rough, uneven lunar surface with mountains, craters, depressions and bulges. He likened it to the surface of the earth with chains of mountains and depths of valleys. With his telescope he also could see the Milky Way, the sunspots and Jupiter's four largest moons, later called in his honor the Galilean moons, out of sixty seven moons that we know of, as of 2014, that orbit Jupiter.

Sir Isaac Newton was born the year that Galileo died, 1647. He observed and reasoned that the same laws of motion and gravity that determine the fall of an apple also determine the motion of the Moon around the earth. That is, gravity works on the moon as it does on the earth.

From the work of Galileo and Newton to today, you can pretty much sum up advances in our knowledge of the Moon and other moons, suns and planets by saying the word telescope. Ever since Galileo built his refracting telescope, this big magnifier has gotten bigger and better, with the Hubble being our supreme achievement. That is, until a bigger and better one is made and paid for.

In 1959 the first pictures were taken by satellite, of the far side of the Moon, the side that we never see, revealing no life, no signs of intelligent beings making things like buildings and no trees or waterways. On April 16, 1999, in a change from its usual peering at the distant universe, the Hubble telescope took a look at the Moon. Hubble was aimed at the Moon's 58-mile-wide impact crater Copernicus. Hubble's crisp, bird's-eye view clearly showed the ray pattern of bright dust ejected out of the crater from over one billion years ago when an asteroid larger than a mile across slammed into the Moon. We were witness to the drama of our Universe, right next to home. And there is always more to learn.

We note that our culture is filled with catchy moon phrases, songs and jokes, movies, fashion, dance and romance, beyond the few I've mentioned, that fill the cracks and crevices of our moonlike brain chambers. But we have heard them all, there's no point in reviewing them. We'll stay on higher ground and stretch up to see and learn whatever we can of that grey ball as it slips away from us into the fading light.

With an adieu, I'll fast forward from a year ago, in 2013, when I wrote much of this essay, to October 9, 2014. An extremely rare kind of total lunar eclipse, that I hope to see, is about to occur in hours as I write in the night. Our moon is going away, but not for too long, thanks to the powers that be in the Universe. The event is called a selenelion or horizontal eclipse. The earth will pass between the sun and the moon, shadowing and eclipsing the moon, taking about four hours from beginning to end. For two to nine minutes at dawn the sun will rise and the moon will set at about the same time. By geometry this should not be possible but it will happen because the atmosphere of the Earth bends the light.

And if the sky is clear, the earth-shadowed moon will shimmer with earth's atmosphere bending light in a beautiful shade of celestial red with maybe a touch of blue. I will see that and the moon's beauty and mysteries will keep stirring the imagination and reverie for the rest of my lifetime and in eons of lives to come as the moon slowly fades away.

NIMBLE

August 2014

A Child's Grown-up Story
Or a Grown-up's Child Story—Be Nimble!

A thousand years ago, in what is today called Great Britain, two words emerged from their now called Old English way of speaking. One word was *naemel* that meant quick to grasp and the other word was *niman* meaning quick at seizing. Both words were useful in the game of chess. The living knights, pawns and kings and the queens and bishops on their real chessboard of English property, where the board game of chess took hold in the 15th century, played a clever, agile game. They were nimble to see all the possible moves. By their quick smarts and spry movements one could outwit the other and take him down with a stone shot or fist wallop or shield grasp. The knight or bishop or rook then took over the new, advanced square of real estate for himself in real life as well as in the chess game on the board. There were no women in the game. The men had nimbly claimed the vast field all to themselves.

Those words, *naemel* and *niman* so aptly described what was called for to perform well in that game of life. The words evolved and as the decades and centuries passed the word *nimble* took hold and won out.

Jack be nimble showed us the word's most recognized usage. Jack came out of oblivion at the turn of the 1700s to the 1800s in a nursery rhyme with lots of questions raised. Was Jack a dog or was he a boy as both were pictured in old texts? Was the candlestick a metaphor for an actual big fire that was dangerous to leap over? Were your children doing child labor when making lace by candlelight during the dark months of the year? Was your great candlestick that was leapt over for game and sport being used for dancing provocatively at English fairs? Was your fortune told by clearing a candle without blowing out the flame good luck? Or was it bad luck because you extinguished the flame? Was Black Jack, an English pirate, who was nimble and clever at escaping authorities in the late 16th Century, the first Jack of Jack be nimble?

Questions unanswered, in the early 1970s, my husband Carl and I heard Don McLean, just feet away from us, on the Dave Letterman TV Show set in NYC, sing the now classic *American Pie*: "Jack be nimble, Jack be quick, Jack Flash sat on a candlestick, 'cause fire is the devil's only friend." Try to make sense of that. Sounds like bad luck to me. But now, Don McClean, alias Jack Flash, is alive and well and, if lucky, nimble in Camden, Maine.

Coming out of common usage today—nimble seamstress, nimble Fred Astaire, nimble bicycle cornering, nimble mathematical calculations, by my figuring, there are three categories of nimbleness. That is, to be nimble in three ways that add up to a healthy, happy, fulfilling life, which I think most of us hope for and have at least partly achieved. Even to the end of our days I think nimbleness is possible!

Ethel's Three Flames of Nimbleness
Be Nimble of Body
Be Nimble of Mind
Be Nimble of Emotions

No. 1: Be Nimble of Body

At age 78, in June 2014, I climbed the rocky path for the four mile round trip to the petroglyphes, carved in rock centuries ago, on the island of Hawaii. With my two grandsons, ages 28 and 14, oldest and youngest of my seven grandchildren born of my three children, we bounced along on our sneakers with the heat, under the noonday sun. The boys leapt from rocky outcropping to more and more heaps of rock. The 14 year-old, a novice of *parkour*, a discipline from the military to move from A to B in the most efficient way and with the fastest momentum possible, nimbly jumped, climbed and propelled himself with daring leaps. My 28 year old took long jumps with a 6'4" frame from one prominence to another, effortlessly. My advancing along this field of multi-faceted rock, with the ancient goal just out of view over the hill, was a bit more cautious in order to maintain balance. But I didn't want to slow up the boys. My sneakers wrapped around a rocky ledge, holding firm and letting go, as all our limbs were doing. Stretching the legs, moving quickly, easily and lightly. Nimble were all our toes, knees, calves, spine, neck, elbows, fingers and shoulders. Nimbly we all moved our joints and connective parts, ligaments and tendons linked and programmed to work and respond to our demands. Nimbleness reigned. Nimbly our bodies responded.

And in the spirited, ready for action terms of this game of life, who was the nimblest of all? The 28 year old noted that he was twice the age of the 14 year old and that I. at 78 years, had a jump of 50 years, exactly a half-century, over him at 28. Perhaps the youngest was the most nimble with less entrenched movement patterns and having muscles, tendons, nerves and blood supply showing less wear, and having more agility present for quickness and ease. But more years make for more time to be in shape, strengthen body parts and to perfect skills and create new neuronal pathways. I'll take that and we can all think young and grow young!

Number 2: Be Nimble of Mind

Be flexible of mind. If your thoughts can be nimble you can also be a nimble listener, catching every word and nuance of someone's talking—has listening become a lost skill? Be able to change a plan. Be ready to change your direction on a dime. Juggle several simultaneous demands on your time with ease and agile attention. Nimbly make the limber neuronal connections in learning to sing a new song and play the piano to showcase how deft and dexterous your mind and fingers are and to build bridges in the brain with music. Be quick to understand all the data thrown your way. Nimbly show your cortical capacity of knowledge and easy access and retrieval of information. Use your gray matter to bring together related thoughts to analyze, collate and draw conclusions, to make inferences nimbly and risk errors with your going out on a limb. Take new and different routes to the same places. Thought and reason keep the brain connections firing and new connections forming. Your brain is inherently nimble, deftly dealing with millions of signals from all five senses every second and responding almost simultaneously, unconsciously and automatically when you lose your balance and, with the SOS of neural circuits of axons and neurons sparking, you quickly avoid a fall. The 100 billion neurons in your nimble noggin cortical tissue are at the ready to fire as in a fire brigade—neuron to neuron to neuron, via axons. This neural network is nimble and made even more nimble and strong with the stimulation of physical and mental exercise. The admonition to use it or lose it is more important than ever through the years. But it's not too late to relearn that poem you memorized in 5th grade for English class or to pick up the violin again. The brain has plasticity, we are happy to have learned in the last couple of decades from researchers and books and real life experience. Plasticity means nimble!

Number 3: Be Nimble of Emotions

Let a rush of changes around you, instead of stressing you out, send you on a captivating ride. When others show negative emotions, be nimble and ready to fill yourself with calmness, peace and humor. Ride the waves. Roll with the punches. If sadness, anger, hurt, guilt, worry, fear or regret creep in, let it go as if you can spin at a turn. Nimbly. Both young and old have a reservoir of nimbleness. Do not invest in bad feelings. They're a waste of your precious time on this earth. Release them. Don't let them hang on and block you. If you're nimble (and you have the capacity!) they will drop away and you are free of all the weight and have the freedom to be even more nimble! Feel how much better it is to live without encumbrances. Even a child or the child in you can understand that concept. Be nimble and live free!

If you can manifest nimbleness in all three areas at any age, kudos to you! I'll go out on a limb nimbly and say "Being nimble is one of the most important traits you can possess in order to get through this life with joy and richness." Even an elephant is nimble and can cross a crevice on a horizontal tree trunk delicately and firmly.

A new species of Tyrannosaurus called Pinocchio Rex (named because of its long snout) has just been unearthed and unveiled by paleontologists in China. Living 66 million years ago it is described by Steve Brusatte of the University of Edinburgh's School of Geosciences as "smaller and more nimble than T-Rex" and "it would have been as deadly as any other tyrannosaur and maybe even a little faster and stealthier" So Pinocchio Rex was more nimble than T Rex and in spite of their huge size both creatures possessed nimbleness to cross the streams and catch their prey.

Cranes have been around since the Eocene Geologic Period, 34 million years ago, and they and their population numbers haven't changed a lot since then. With 99 percent of species that ever existed on earth now being extinct, how do you explain the cranes' survival? The answer is that they have been very highly adaptable (according to *Smithsonian March 2014*). It took being nimble to stay alive. They are rare creatures that have flown away from inhospitable environments and diminishing food supply and moved on to friendlier places for millennia. They don't seem to make a lot of enemies (bears, coyotes, wolves and hawks eat them, though the cranes themselves are mostly vegetarian), certainly not an enemy of me or me of them up close in the Sandhill Crane Preserve in central Wisconsin. Remarkable describes their appearance with long, thin legs and necks and powerful wings and their strong traits of staying with and caring for the flock. Nimble is the reason for the Sandhill crane's impressive survival for 10 million years!

Elves, the objects of children's and adult's affection, are of a mystical and mythical folklore tradition. They are a varied species from country to country, from book to book and modern day movie to movie. You have the license to write up your own description of what you want an elf to be. Appearing in Scandinavian lore the *alf* or *troll* is tiny with wings and lives in a rose blossom. Other countries describe them as taller or smaller than humans, friendly or not, dangerous in making you dance to your death or just being tricksters and sneaky. The traits that most elves have in common are living a long time up to a millennium, having long pointy ears, living in nature's caves, forests and dark woods and being attached and color matched to the natural world. But the longest-lived, most observed quality that elves possess in common, me thinks, is to be nimble. They move nimbly. They think nimbly and so muster up mischief, cause danger and create surprise. But, what about other mystical creatures, such as gnomes, fairies, trolls, pixies and leprechauns? Some have been called nimble in written stories. But, they all must be nimble, as a magician is, to transform the world to magic.

A world away from the natural, supernatural and superhuman are businesses that, besides sometimes including Nimble as part of their trademarked name (how can nimble be claimed legally when there is an essence of freedom in this word? It's an oxymoron!), need to be nimble to accommodate to the business environment and to flourish and grow. Their working strategy is to expect change, adapt to change and then benefit from it with the best sales and profit. They call themselves nimble in accomplishing that goal.

And in the arts, pliant clay in the quick hands of a proficient potter nimbly becomes a creation of art—all parts are qualities of nimbleness. There will always be the nimble fingers of a pianist, the nimble body of a ballet dancer and the nimble thinking of an architect, plus the nimbleness of feelings of any of us to cry when someone does you a kind deed and your heart is touched.

It's worth keeping nimbleness and its goodness in your life. Emulate nimbleness around you. Read a book with a nimble plot. Catch a ride on a jungle jeep and keep your balance while standing in the back of the open jeep as it climbs steepness beyond belief—I've done it on the island of Bora Bora in the Pacific.

Nimble has come a long way. Bred in early language, navigating across seas, hibernating in nursery rhymes and whimsical tales and showing up here and there like a fresh breeze. There was need for this word. Its hatching and longevity have been a trip that can alone be described as nimble. Just as the word itself survived, the nimblest stay alive.

Charles Darwin said, "It is not the strongest of the species that survives, not the most intelligent, but the one most responsive to change."

That might make us the nimblest of all!

Ethel Erickson Radmer

ONWARD

Chapter 11 from *Conversations with Carl: My Journey Through Grief*
© 2006 Ethel Erickson Radmer

There are things I want to do. I have a life ahead of me, as well as the present moment to relish. Singing, for one, and whatever else comes up on my spacious pallet of possibilities. Now that the one-year mark has passed, I somehow feel a little freer and ready to move on. You have told me many times from your spirit world to be happy and enjoy life and I've tried and partially succeeded. But I want more pleasure out of life and less angst.

On day one of my new year, I meet a new male friend, as we had planned, for coffee and we talk about a myriad of things, but especially about taking walks and climbs. In the evening I climb that long hill to UCSF and audition for a choral group. Yes, audition! How brave I am singing new music alone and with several others, unaccompanied, with tricky timing and note changes, on the stage in Cole Hall. I've sung alone and in groups before, but it has been a long time, and I'm feeling my sea legs. My voice is a little shaky. But Carl, I passed!

What joy it is to be part of this group, The San Francisco Choral Society. The music is majestic, ageless and brilliant.

Brahm's "German Requiem." Haydn's "Lord Nelson Mass in D Minor." Mozart's "Mass in C." Rachmaninoff's "Vespers" and Britten's'

"Rejoice in The Lamb." Marek Jasinski's "Alleluja" and Morton Lauridsen's "Ubi Caritas Et Amor." It thrills me to even say the names of these composers and works. We sing A cappella works by Pablo Casals' "O Vos Omnes," Johannes Brahms' "Darthulas Grabesgesang" and Moses Hogan's "Ev'ry Time I Feel The Spirit." Over time we do homage to those composers and many others in Davies Symphony Hall, Saint Ignatius Church and other churches and even under the dome of City Hall. And my family comes to bask in the beauty. I wink surreptitiously to them in the balcony.

I love the music. It is so reflective of all of my senses, my ruminations and my appreciation. I feel grief, sadness and yearning, and reverence, love and glory in the singing. It radiates to me and through me and from me.

Brahms himself said, "Now I am consoled ... I feel like an eagle, soaring ever higher and higher." Oh Brahms, I am so in tune with you! I feel so consoled with the beauty of the music. I am floating to new heights, perhaps to where your spirits dwell. Carl, you're in good company!

It is Sunday and Tammy called to invite me to go with the three of them to the tidal pools at Moss Beach. Dave drives us south as far as the Half Moon Bay Airport, where we turn toward the ocean and park. With Melia being carried in a baby backpack on Dave's shoulders, we head into the cold, penetrating wind off the water. Just south of us is Mavericks off Pillar Point, where surfers from around the world compete. They come with a day's notice if the waves are high, in the winter. But it is late January, just north of the point and we are alone. We are wedged between the water and the eroding cliff, so typical of California beaches. The tide is out to reveal the tidal pools, uncommon treasures on the coastline. A ways out, the waves are crashing over large rocks exposed in low tide, making a rhythmic, thunderous sound. There are a few brown seals, hanging out on the rocks, warming in the sun.

We walk in the sand where the shallow pools are, cautiously skittering over the rough rocks that are very slippery with green, almost moss-like seaweed. Our feet and our hands are numbed as we test the very cold clear waters. How in the moment we are! The sandy floors of the scattered but contiguous pools are covered with crushed, glittering shells, iridescent colors sparkling in the sun. Orange and green starfish, tentacles reaching, are well secured to the rocks. Beautiful sea anemones, turquoise and purple and burgundy, are floating just below the surface of the water, attached underneath to the reef.

There is even more life! Dipping down, we see small fish darting around and little crabs scurrying about. A conflux of mussels, blue and black, are clustered around each other. Strands of flat, fibrous, shiny kelp float aimlessly. We look, we feel, we breathe in the cold air and feel warmed by the sun. Time stands still. I don't know if minutes or hours have gone by.

Life, in all its glory. Nature with its mystery. Beauty, not of our doing. We are in rapture. Slowly, we walk to the car. Tammy, Dave, Melia and I have been intimate today with a fascinating, intricate seascape and natural beauty, so real, but almost beyond belief. I'll feast for time to come.

How fortunate I am, Carl. Prodigious gifts are in my life. I treasure my family. I can take in beauty with all my senses. I have talent from some power beyond myself to create in exciting and gratifying ways. Life is good, even without you, my dearest, no longer nearest, except when I feel your spirit, which I do now. "I am glad for you, Ethel.

Be brave. You are doing just what I knew you would do. Exploring and getting the most you could out of life. I embrace you, my love."

It's Valentine's Day. I feel tugs for you, Carl, in my heart and thoughts. The memories are strong. We were lovers and I miss you greatly. My urge, though, is not to bemoan, but to be active and take my almost daily walk on Ocean Beach. I walk twice today, once with a friend and once alone. When walking alone, I was thinking about my pink quartz heart, that my massage therapist suggested I buy. I decided, while walking, that I would have a hole drilled in the top (ouch!), a fixing put in and a chain and wear it as a pendant, close to my heart. Pink quartz conveys calm and tranquility and loving myself, sentiments I feel and want. Just then, something written in the sand caught my eye and I walked back to look. A large heart was drawn, with these words inside, "I Love Me." Wow! Did someone read my thoughts? I have instant confirmation! Yes! I DO love myself. Sometimes, I am hard on myself, replaying tapes of hurtful times. There is no use in that. It's good to be reminded to be kind to my sometimes, fragile self, to be easy and be good to me. I look at my red turtleneck that I have on to commemorate the day and I take in the heartfelt message.

Randy and Bonnie and dear little Lauren had me over to their house just around the corner of the block from my apartment at the end of the day. We exchanged hugs and kisses and valentines. Lauren had drawn a red heart on white paper with a two and a half years old child's script, "I love you, Grandma Ethel!" It has been a veritable love fest today!

Kate Michelman, President of NARAL, NationalAbortion Rights Action League, talked at the Commonwealth Club and I attended. Now, I am not for abortion by any stretch, but I do want to keep it out of the back allies and let doctors perform it legally, when needed, without their hands being tied. I worked hard and was a leader for this cause, in the '70s and '80s. I spoke with Kate about working in the trenches. She's a lovely person and she wondered why I came to San Francisco. When I said my husband died, her sweetness and understanding showed. "I am so sorry," she offered. And then, on learning of my present life, she said, "Congratulations on making a new life for yourself!" Thank you, Kate. I feel so good with that. I did create a whole new life and it's a good one.

And that reminds me, Carl. I am tired of causes. I did my bit for so many worthy groups, through the years. Let others take over. Now, I take pleasure in squeezing the most out of and into my new life. Curiosity is a driving force. I want to learn everything about everything and do whatever I can and want to do and haven't done.

The lectures at UC Medical are regular fare for my appetite. I just heard a talk on naturopathy, which I do know a lot about. What interested me was the story of the speaker's husband, a medical doctor, who had lymphoma. They went wherever they could find alternative healing and also did chemotherapy and a bone marrow transplant. It was a positive experience for them. What we did, Carl, was a positive experience for us too. The doctor with lymphoma died after 10 years. You, dear husband, died four months after you were diagnosed with cancer. I wanted a day more, a week more, a month more, or a year. Is our time on this earth never enough?

AARP thinks you are still here, as do numerous money management groups and financial institutions, no matter what I tell them. I have tried and tried to cancel your AARP membership (you knew I didn't like associating with the word 'old' or with the single-minded politics of the group, which was 'we're entitled to all the benefits we can get' kind of thinking), and the bulletins and promotions keep coming. They and others have even tracked down your new abode, which is mine, though you never lived in San Francisco. I announce to all, "Your new address is the stars!"

I occasionally feel my parental roots, which are Swedish. Remember our two visits to Sweden, Carl, one time with our pre-teen children? We were immersed in family. Such kindness and hospitality emanated from them and I used my very halting Swedish to talk with my mother's cousin and my aunt, Elizabet. Here in San

Francisco, to get a flavor of the Scandinavian, I took MUNI Bus 43 to the water and attended a monthly Swedish Sunday service at the Norwegian Seaman's Church. I felt like I was in Sweden! My voice was full and strong as I sang longingly, hymns in Swedish: "Tryggare Kan Ingen Vara" (Children of the Heavenly Father), "Dag For Dag Ogenblick I Sander" (Day By Day and With Each Passing Moment), and "Jag Har En Vin Som Alskar Mig" (I Have A Friend Who Loveth Me). I admired the table spread of kringlor, sma kaka, brod and smor and syltt and ost. Bowls for berries were filled with jordgubba and lingonmousse, A blond woman served kaffe with socker and gradde. I mixed with people that had a strong resemblance to each other. The view of the Bay from our elegant space in the Marina, partway up the hill, was calm and picture perfect. I took in the serene splendor.

But, even with that savorous experience I confess to feeling lonely. It comes on me sometimes. I remember the fun of the past with you and I want you here in the present. It's hard to get over 39 years of togetherness, Carl. You see my sad heart, I know you do. I almost know what you are going to say. "Ethel, we're reading each other's thoughts. I see your tears. Let them come. It's good to open up and let the sadness out. My love for you is greater than ever. Feel a kiss. I'm with you."

Oh Carl that's more than I even hoped for. It means so much to me. That is you. Please, hang around for awhile. I need that especially now, in my melancholic state of mind. I just knew you would answer. Thanks and love from me.

I'm feeling my roots again, this time in Wisconsin, our birth state, where we earned our degrees, married and raised our children to school age. A couple of years before you died we looked for lake property on the Eagle River Chain of Lakes in the Wisconsin Northwoods. We had sold our East Coast properties and were free of ownership ties. Years ago in the Adirondack Mountains of New

York, we had built a unique smart-looking boat house and a bedroom and screen porch addition to a lake cabin. Creating, designing and building was our thing and we were good at it. Tempted with new Wisconsin terrain, we had such fun designing yet more lake homes, but we never bought any land.

Well, I'm dreaming again for both of us. My sister found land for sale and I flew out and looked at it. Within a day I signed the papers and it's mine. There are luxurious tall pine filling the sloping lot to the waters of Hiawatha, facing the setting sun and an orange glow rippling across the lake's reflective surface. It is my flight of fancy. Maybe someday I'll build a place and maybe I won't. But it's all my own. I want to dream.

I'm doing good things for myself and treating myself well. Such nice experiences I'm having in this new life. I imagine you Carl being with me on almost all these occasions and really do feel your spirit. It is so real, so natural and comfortable, You are a cozy presence. And Carl, I am realizing happiness without you. I know you want that for me. My artist's palette is filling with living colors and there is room for more.

Ethel Erickson Radmer

PIANO

May 2014

It is a love affair of the heart. When I was a toddler and could barely reach the keys, I fell in love with the piano. With my first pressing of the ivories with my long, baby-skin fingers, a sound came out and it was music to my ever-so-receptive, virgin ears. The romance has lasted a lifetime of many decades and it has stayed passionate and true. And the pleasure still erupts in my being when I hear and feel the music of this remarkable, best known and most played of all keyboard musical instruments that are around. The piano.

Romance is the word. A fascinating, mysterious and adventurous affair with the piano and music has carried me through this unpredictable, event-filled time on earth that we all have a chance at. And the romance of that time for me was poignantly expressed back in the 19th century by Renoir, one of the impressionistic painters of Europe in what was called the Romantic Period (from the mid-18th century through the 19th century). Romanticism flourished then in the visual arts, in music and in literature. Feel the romance of the poetry of Mary Wollstonecraft Shelley and of William Blake! Hear the romantic music of Chopin, Liszt and Schumann, all pianists as well as composers! And see romanticism shining in the paintings of Monet, Degas and Renoir! For all those writers, musicians and artists it was a time of setting free their emotional expression, such as joy, sadness and awe on an even bigger palette of 'creating from nothingness' and filled with a new and restless spirit that infused Romanticism.

Pierre-August Renoir was considered an originator of the Impressionistic style, the visual arts movement that grew during the Romantic period, influencing literature and music as well as art. In the middle of his career, 1892 to be precise, Renoir painted in oil and sketched in pastel a series of five paintings—all the same scene and pretty close to identical and now found in galleries and private collections in Europe and the United States, called *Young Girls at the Piano*. This gorgeous, ethereal painting shows two young sisters, one sitting on the piano bench with her left hand fingers on the music and her right hand fingers on the keys and the other sister standing and leaning close with her hand outstretched to the sheet of music on the piano music rest. The girls wear long dresses, one of light pink and the other of white with a blue sash. The whole painting exudes a glowing show of color, intimacy, and vibrant light. The girls are making music and both the girls could be me.

The sisters' unmistakable intensity of their interest in the music radiates now to my young mind of long ago. The curiosity, the mystery, the infatuation are all there as I felt it in those innocent days of youth that seemed without end. The piano I played was an upright piano and had center stage in our living room, but it came used and in need of tuning and repair and later went as firewood when it couldn't be fixed anymore. But have no fear; a flawed piano was what I knew and was grateful for and I could also play my grandmother's piano on her farm, the Baptist Church piano and all my friends' pianos whenever the chance was there. Those were the days of almost every house in the town of Whitehall having a piano grace their living room or, in the case of my friend Patty, a music room! Imagine a beautiful, windowed space with elegant settees for just listening to someone perform on brass and reed instruments that, if around, usually sat in their cases and the oak stained, upright piano, with a white lace doily spread out on top, standing tall against the entrance wall. It was a scene for Renoir and the two sisters and I was in it playing that piano!

I'll tell you about the piano through the eyes of a child growing up, full of questions and discoveries while gaining my own storehouse of knowledge. I was pretty much on my own in my piano adventure and was able to mostly figure it all out by myself. None of my six older siblings gave much if any attention to our upright piano, while I, the seventh and last in the family brood, was in awe. I taught myself to play by ear and to read music and to make up my own combination of notes. I wondered what is inside this wooden piano case that makes for a sound. What and where are all the parts? How do they work together? I asked myself a thousand more questions through the years. And then I made discoveries by playing notes with those long fingers. I could tell by the sound of tunes that I knew where I should go up or down on the keyboard and I made new music and new sound with a *joie de vivre.*

The most obvious and important thing to see, figure out and learn to play, is the keyboard. The keyboard is full of keys all lined up in a row for my child's comprehension. I knew what an octave was because the sound of the top key of an octave and bottom key resonate the same to my ears, but the top is a higher sound than the bottom. I counted 8 notes or keys played in an octave. I counted 7 octaves, plus it may have had 3 more keys at the bottom in what is called a minor third (some older pianos did not have the minor third but newer ones did) on the piano keyboard and a total of 88 keys. 52 of those keys are white and 36 are black. The black keys are shorter than the white keys and are located between the white keys and spaced apart in groups of 2 and 3. The white keys have letter names. Middle C is slightly to left of the middle of the keyboard.

The next white key up and to the right from Middle C is D, the next are E, F, G and then A, B, C and the pattern is repeated to the top key C. The same pattern is followed from the bottom note A and on up to where we started at middle C. The black keys can be called sharps or flats depending on the key in which the music is played (as shown in the key signature drawn at the beginning of the staff in written music). An example of this is calling one black key either A-sharp or B-flat—that is the black key just below the white key B is B-flat and that same black key just above the white key A is called A-sharp, again depending on the key in which the music is written. The white keys were made of wood and capped with strips of ivory from elephant tusks and molars until we became publically aware of the diminishing elephant population and then plastic materials started being used. The black keys are made of ebony wood.

Using both hands, I learned to play the different scales, playing each piano key of an octave in different letter keys, such as playing a scale in the key of C or in the key of F-sharp. Playing chords, which is playing several notes that sound good together with one hand, followed naturally for me. The sound of chords was so much richer than a single note and led to more fun places in my playing. With chords there were major and minor keys to explore and chords gave different notes to sing in an ensemble of voices. With that information, I took off on playing a familiar tune in my head, especially hymns, where I most often sang while playing, or playing my own music out of my head and into my ears and knowing how to play a tune in my head in any key you picked—known as playing by ear. As the music becomes more complex, the terminology list to describe it increases, the musical concepts multiply and moving your fingers and hands around the keyboard becomes more challenging and fun. But it's worth the work for the sound you get. And the sound is what I savored as a kid and savor still. I was not an aficionado of piano sound then—you need to hear a lot of sounds from dozens or hundreds of pianos to start to note differences and appreciate what might be more pleasing to the ear than another sound.

I learned somewhere along the way in music class in school, decades ago when every grade in my Wisconsin elementary school had a music teacher come into class two or more times a week to teach us how to sing music a cappella, using a starting note from a small pitch pipe that she blew, or accompanied by a piano that many classrooms possessed. Or, I learned it on my own that our modern piano was invented by an Italian named Bartolomeo Cristofori (1655–1731). He called his piano a pianoforte. Going backwards in time, the pianoforte was preceded by the clavichord and the harpsichord in the 17th century. During the Middle Ages, the lute, harp and viol were some of the string instruments made and played. Even earlier the strings were struck in hammered dulcimers. Each preceding string instrument in history was simpler in every way than what was to follow. Our modern piano is essentially the same instrument as the pianoforte was over hundreds of years. It has stood the test of time.

The piano, showing its versatility, is placed in three musical categories. It is called a keyboard instrument, a string instrument and a percussion instrument. One or another of those features were present in all medieval musical instruments that were made centuries ago and are forerunners to the piano. The pipe organ uses a keyboard to drive air or wind through pipes and produce sound and it also has been used for centuries. Its origins are traced back to the 3rd century BC in Ancient Greece and to the hydraulis, a pipe organ blown by air from a waterfall or other force of water, no bellows needed. The string instruments were many and diverse throughout the ages. A percussion instrument is sounded by being struck or scraped with a beater or hammer, as a hammer strikes the strings in a piano. The oldest musical instruments are considered to be percussive, such as drums and shakers. So the piano incorporates all three features: keyboard, strings and percussion.

Besides the keyboard, the other obvious outside feature of the piano to my curious eyes, were the pedals. Three of these metal pads, flat with a curved shape, sat near the floor, extending on posts that are attached to the piano cabinet and connect to the inside workings. The sustain pedal, on the right, holds the sound. The damper pedal, on the left, softens the sound and the sostenuto pedal, in the middle, sustains common notes among different chords. I experimented to see how useful they were to use.

The next thing for me to take in as a child was all the inside parts that our upright piano was made of and how they fit and work together. I saw the parts by standing up on the wooden piano bench that my mother had built, lifting the top lid back on its hinges and peering in. But a better view opened up, with both the piano and its parts and me standing up in a vertical position, when the piano tuner, on a rare visit, took off the big front wooden rectangle. You could figure out most of the workings just by looking at the inside parts and striking the ivory keys at the same time. After finishing the University and getting married, I bought my first grand piano where the parts are mostly horizontal within a harp-shaped wooden case.

The prominent and biggest thing you see inside is a harp-shaped iron frame or plate, securely fastened to the inside of the back part of the piano case. There are up to 230 steel strings stretched from one end of this frame to the other end. There are about 170 pounds of tension coming from each string. So adding it up, the very durable iron frame holds 40,000 pounds of tension from all its strings. That is a lot of stress and all parts need to be strong and held firmly in place. The longest and thickest strings stretched on the 'harp' are the bass notes. The shortest and thinnest strings are the highest notes. The strings lose their brightness and tone with age and beyond twenty years probably need to be replaced. The strings are the 'voice' of the piano, just as your vocal cords vibrate to sing and make music.

Underneath the iron plate and the strings is the soundboard. It has a curvature that stretches across the width and length of the piano. It is made of spruce. When the strings are struck, the sound travels through a wooden bridge that is attached to the soundboard. The bridge supports the strings and transmits the strings' vibrations to the soundboard which resonates and amplifies the sound with the help of naturally moving air.

Pressing the piano keys activates the hammers. The hammers hit the strings and make them resonate. The hammers are made of hard maple and have rounded felt heads made of compressed layers of fine wool. The sound quality of the piano has a lot to do with the hardness of the hammers. Soft hammers produce a dull sound. Hard hammers make for a bright sound. Dampers also have felt pads. While resting on the strings (when you use the damper pedal) dampers stop most of the sound from resonating. When the damper is raised off the strings, the string can again vibrate and produce full sound. The high notes don't have dampers because the short strings don't resonate that much and what sound is left softly fades away. You can see the tuning pins in the front of the piano's internal works. It makes for easy access for tuning. The pins are secured into and through the iron plate and into the pin block. Each piano string is wrapped around a separate tuning pin. One key might have up to three strings on the high notes, two strings on the lower notes and one on the very low notes for a total of up to 230 strings. The back-posts, made of spruce, give support to the soundboard and the rest of the piano.

And finally we have the action. It is the mechanism that connects the keys to the strings. It is intricate and complex and composed of up to 10,000 parts. When I bought my second grand piano at a shop in New York City, I played several pianos to see how I liked the action. That is critical for a purchase. You trust all the parts to be the best and in fine working order. But you really need to see how it 'feels' when you play. Is it tight and resistant or slow or quickly responsive or loose to your pressing the keys? And of course there is the sound. What sounds best to you? Can you live with it? But the sound of the flawed piano I grew up with would still be mesmerizing music to my ears.

For my inner child's understanding, I'll sum up very simply how the piano works. You press down on a key on the keyboard. This makes a hammer inside the piano strike a string. The string makes a sound. The pitch of the sound depends on the string's tension and its length. Different pitches make for music. End of story.

So, there you have the piano. There is much to know and much to enjoy when that grand instrument is listened to and when it is played. Yes, there is playing to do! And there is technique to learn. In my case, I taught myself how to play. There was barely one teacher along the way for a brief time who commented that I was her first pupil to make up music (however simple) and to write it down. My hand position came from my instincts and what felt good and from watching others. It's probably best, though, to get some attention from someone in the know. But go with whatever you're comfortable with. Watch how a jazz musician might pounce on a key. Notice how the church pianist seems to hold her hands strained up high above the keyboard. Your quickness, flexibility and strength and other skills might be worked on or may come naturally. If you play a piece enough times your arm, hand and finger muscles retain a memory of how and where to play and you may have the piece memorized and not need the music. You are playing by heart! Selections of music come from volumes of classical, jazz, religious, contemporary and other genres of music that we have hardly begun to explore. There are composers to know from centuries ago and on up to the modern age. Ideas are hatching for new piano music this very moment.

To learn more and clarify what the music is all about and to describe the composers and the kind of music that you play and to understand the complexity of music theory is for another time, or as a piano teacher would write down and say, "This is your assignment for your next lesson, dear."

As I was playing the Baldwin grand, that became mine, in the New York City piano shop, the guy told me that some famous pianist (I don't remember who) had played that grand in concert. So, I've had visions ever since of Martha Argerich playing Maurice Ravel, or Claudio Arrau playing Liszt, or Vladimir Ashkenazy playing Schumann, and of Daniel Barenboim playing Mendelsohn, all pianists who, by chance, have 'A' names and one 'B' like the first letter key A and next key B on the keyboard going up, and all of those well-known pianists playing composers of the Romantic era, Renoir's time and influence, in concert at Avery Fisher Hall in Lincoln Center and I've had visions of their nimble fingers playing the piano that I bought and treasure and have passed on to my daughter and her children. I want to keep the pianists coming in future generations.

And I tell the children about the piano through the eyes of a child.

Ethel Erickson Radmer

QUARK

March 2014

My husband was on the hunt for quarks. It was in the middle of the 1950s leading to the mid-1960s when a team of scientists in the Midwest were, with total intellectual freedom and with bare-bones financing and without the heavy hand of government encumbrances, were on the cusp of developing accelerators. MURA was their name, spelled out as *Midwestern University Research Association*, a collaboration of fifteen universities and headquartered in Madison, Wisconsin in the old brown brick Nash Garage on University Avenue. And the group, including names like Kerst, Young, Symon, Cole, Mills, Jones, Swenson, and Radmer and with visits from the likes of the 1922 Nobel Prize winner in Physics, Niels Bohr, spending time with the team around their Radial Sector Model in 1958, always calling that place of their work "the garage."

Of course accelerator work and particle physics were going on in other parts and places at the same time—at Brookhaven in NY, at SLAC in California, at Fermilab in Illinois, as well as in Switzerland, Japan and dozens of other sites. And it was earlier in time, in the 1920s and 1930s, that physics researchers gave us the building blocks of physics inquiry and knowledge of particles of matter and in the 1940's the know-how of the power of the atom to put in a bomb and use two of them on Nagasaki and Hiroshima in

Japan and thus call an end to WWII. After the war in the mid-forties, the mad-furies of the weaponry having come to a halt, physicists could again direct their attention and resources to pure physics and the quest for finding the fundamental particles of the universe.

It was a heady time. The intellectual drive was enormous. The team at MURA would have said, "It's FUN, no kidding!" To say these physicists and engineers were curious was putting it mildly. The energy level was high and they were a team that wanted to DO it. They were on the hunt to find that smallest bit of matter. And how do you find out what something is made of? Take it apart! But you can't just 'will-apart' an atom. We did know about molecules, the smallest physical unit of an element or compound, by the 19th Century and way back to 490 to 430 BC we got a clue about elements from Empedocles, a Greek philosopher. He imagined fundamental elements like fire, earth, air and water as well as (importantly!) 'forces' of attraction and repulsion making it possible for the elements to interact.

So we broke up the molecules into atoms in the early 19th Century (John Dalton gets the credit for suggesting the idea of atoms being the smallest particle) and then we tore apart the atoms to reveal a nucleus (protons and neutrons) plus electrons orbiting the nucleus. But there was further work to do. We hoped that all wars were at an end for all time but protons and electrons weren't the end of our search. It seemed that what it would take to find out the inner works of those particles was to break them apart in a cataclysmic way. Smash them with the strongest force possible! Hit them with the highest energy you could muster up.

And so accelerators or smashers, described as atomic, linear, circular, particle, and hadron accelerators, were conceived of in order to speed up the particles (*electrons* filled the beam in the accelerators Carl worked on) to as near the *speed of light* as possible.

A beam of particles was injected into the computer ring or linear cavity, speeded up with MW or megawatts of electric power and the help of magnets to 'focus' the beam, and when it got at max capability to produce near light speed it hit a target such as metal foil. *Or* beams of electron or positron particles would be made to collide with each other in a two-way or colliding beam accelerator, but housed in one ring, which the physicists and engineers at MURA in large part developed first. Importantly they found *useful* colliding beams—before any other scientists did.

Computation of data, measuring effects and forces of all kinds within the accelerator, proving existence of chaos in digital computation and in synchrotron-radiation rings, and the list goes on, were all assisted by computers of the day, such as they were, that is many decades ago. The MURA lab used an IBM 704, the first mass produced computer. Like other computers in the 1950s and 1960s, it was big and bulky and took up huge amounts of space, possessed much less function capability and memory and far less speed than what we take for granted in a 21st century computer that is smaller than our lap and able to do calculations beyond belief.

But in all of the above-mentioned areas of computation including the human group 'cell' of brain and drive, free-wheeling intellect and creative thinking, MURA led the way among all the other accelerators in innovation and in the innovative accomplishments that were later incorporated in other accelerators around the globe. With the work at many accelerators, particles smaller than protons, neutrons and electrons (in the atom) were found, but no one then could find the smoking gun to prove that quarks existed.

Call them what you will and give them a name if you wish; this particle *quark* is a basic building block of matter. It is thought to be *the* fundamental particle. The name *quark* almost doesn't matter except to define and differentiate. I would have imagined the concept as a cave-kid living in caveman days. The wondering, the philosophical postulating of what is the teeniest, tiniest bit that we can get to, to break down to, in that stone that is impeding our path or the smallest part in the grain of dirt on our cave floor... or ...is it *infinitesimal* with no end to the cutting finer and finer, I would have asked, with no end in sight. And the irony of it is—we will never *see* a quark, by most physicists thinking, because one quark cannot be isolated alone and so it cannot be directly observed. But we still know by the evidence left that they exist.

For the sake of information, history and ease of discourse, the word *quark* was claimed and attached to this most fundamental of particles by physicists Gell-Mann and separately by Zweig in 1964. Gell-Mann also gets credit for naming *The Eightfold Way*, a sort of chart like the Table of Elements which gave evidence by nature's organization (yes—the cosmos can make the claim for possession! It's *nature's* invention!) and by the gaps on the eightfold chart for this elusive particle. When physicists realized that the existence of underlying fundamental particles could explain the eightfold pattern, the *idea* of quarks was born. And independently, Yuval Ne'eman came up with the same theory as Gell-Mann that organized all the particles into families with properties mathematically the same as those of a "group of eight" in abstract algebra.

The evidence for the quark was gathering and building up for decades. And a lot of scientists could make a claim for forming their theories, finding their data and reaching their conclusions first. Whether or not the team at MURA used the word 'quark'—it was a 'fundamental particle' to them—they knew that they were looking for the unknown. And they discovered the physics underpinning of contemporary particle accelerators along the way—that is they accomplished well more than a dozen impactful things that future accelerators, including the big Hadron Accelerator at CERN, incorporated into their own advanced and continuing advancing models. Knowledge builds on knowledge and sometimes people or groups get credit and sometimes they don't.

And, in addition to their work on accelerators in Madison, I'll give credit to Carl and the rest of the MURA team on the top of Mount Evans and at Echo Lake (high altitude and less atmosphere to block cosmic rays) in Colorado throughout the 1960s for theorizing, designing and building equipment, accumulating and recording data and overall executing a scientific project for a gathering of cosmic rays from the universe! A small number of the huge number of cosmic rays that fill the cosmos can make their way through the earth's atmosphere and maybe, just maybe a quark would be found slipping through our atmospheric shield and leave evidence or a marking or a trace of its existence. These engineers and physicists never found convincing evidence of the quark, for all their looking on the mountain top. Though, the data may still be looked at today with more updated (in experience and technology) eyes. I do remember the guys (yes, all the scientists on the team were men as was all of physics then with very few exceptions) talking at length about searching for *quarks*. I think they got a jump on Gill-Mann's 1964 'quark' announcement by at least a couple of years.

Back in the denser atmosphere of Madison and to MURA's FFAG or Fixed Field Alternating Gradient Accelerator (which Keith Symon, on the MURA team says they invented), to Berkeley's Circular Cyclotron until 2002, to Brookhaven National Laboratory or BNL and their Relativistic Heavy Ion Collider which was designed to research *quark-gluon plasma* and was the world's most powerful particle accelerator up to 2008 in Upton, NY on Long Island, to the Cambridge Electron Accelerator, a joint undertaking of MIT and Harvard and begun in 1956, to Michigan State's cyclotron (variation on atom smasher), to Fermilab's 200-MeV linac in Batavia, Illinois, to LAMPF in Los Alamos, to Iowa State's Betatron (another accelerator variation), to SLAC's linear (straight line for beam) at Stanford in California from 1966 on to the present day in 2014 (where Carl's and my son, Randall is on staff), to Purdue's bubble-chamber (filled with liquid hydrogen to detect electrically charged particles moving through it), to CERN's Proton Synchrotron in Geneva, Switzerland in 1959 and leading up to the collaboration of 10,000 scientists and engineers from over 100 countries and 100s of universities and laboratories to build the largest and most powerful particle collider in the world, the Large Hadron Collider known as the LHC, built in a tunnel 17 miles in circumference and starting operations in 2009, are some of the accelerators that existed then and now and all working to hunt for the unknown and perhaps find the illusive quark or to discover other elementary particles.

Decades after the 1950s and 1960s' flourishing of accelerators, in 2012, what became known as the Higgs particle or *Higgs boson* (named after the pioneer in theorizing the boson, theoretical physicist Peter Higgs) was discovered at the LHC and then the observation was confirmed in 2013. The boson is considered a fundamental particle but it is bigger than and I will say "not as fundamental as the sub-atomic particle *quark*." A boson consists of a combination of quarks. Though ever so briefly, the quark *does* exist by itself and *cannot* be divided any further. That sets the quark apart from the boson that *can* divide into quarks. So a quark is as fundamental as we can get with what we know now.

All of these accelerators I've named and more were in various stages of being worked on, operating and producing data for physics and making practical applications in medicine through the 1960s and beyond. In 1964 President Johnson turned down the MURA proposal for a major high-energy research accelerator in the Midwest. It was a big disappointment but the team carried on with their experiments for a couple more years until after 1966, when the accelerator work was shifted by the University of Wisconsin to the Physical Sciences Laboratory. The men scattered to other labs and accelerators or to the corporate world, as Carl did. But their work was not in vain. Their discoveries have led to more revelations. And with a nod to Carl in the book *Innovation Was Not Enough: A History of the Midwestern Universities Research Association* ©2010 by Jones, Mills, Sessler, Symon and Young, Carl Radmer was credited with making numerous important contributions (designing and building) to making beam, building extraction kickers and power supplies for betatron accelerating cores, high-power radio frequency amplifiers for linacs and much more. And more and more evidence has come in that the quark must exist and that other sub-atomic particles do exist. Though (again) it has never been directly observed or found in isolation and probably never will be, we expect the quark will soon find a more solid place on the charts.

Now that researchers know more about the quark and can calculate its existence and see the evidence, it's time to describe what is. And part of what is known is knowing what other sub-atomic particles there are and what distinguishes them from each other. We're getting a taste of how all the particles fit into the scheme of things. And, all together now, what can we learn about the structure of matter?

The *standard model* of particle physics (theory agreed on by scientists around the world) says that matter can be divided into these three building blocks: 1. *Fermions* (named after the physicist Enrico Femi). 2. *Hadrons* (as in Large *Hadron* Collider in Geneva). 3. *Bosons* (as in the *Higgs boson*).

The first of the three building blocks, *Fermions* are divided into *leptons* and *quarks*. As a fundamental particle, a quark cannot be broken up into other particles. The second building block *hadrons* are composite particles such as *protons* and *neutrons*. Hadrons are made up of combinations of quarks. That is, quarks combine to form composite particles. Since a quark can never be directly observed or found in isolation, it is only within hadrons, where quarks combine, that we can attempt to study the quark. The two types of hadrons are *mesons* (one quark and one antiquark) and *baryons* (three quarks).

The third building block of matter, *Bosons*, are particles that carry *forces*—go back again to 450 BC when Empedocles imagined fundamental elements and *forces* of attraction and repulsion for the elements to interact. *Forces* can be divided into four kinds of fundamental forces. 1. *Strong* holds the nucleus of the atom together. 2. *Weak* is active in radioactive decay. 3. *Electromagnetism* is for interaction between charged particles. 4. *Gravity* is an attractive force based on mass and distance. There are four known *bosons*: *gluon* and *W* and *Z* and *photon*. A fifth, *graviton* has been proposed but not found.

Going back to the first of three building blocks of matter, *fermions* distinguish between matter (*leptons* and *quarks*) and *antimatter* (we'll get to that later). *Leptons* are of at least two kinds: *electron* and *neutrino*. This brings us to characteristics of the *quark*, the centerpiece of my writing.

A quark is described as an elementary particle and the most fundamental constituent of matter. It is extremely small. It participates in the *strong* nuclear force (of the 4 forces listed). It has a fractional electrical charge. A quark will combine with another quark so quickly that they have not been seen alone. There are six classifications or 'flavors' of quark, each with a different charge and a different mass, and with surprisingly simple names: *down, up, strange, charm, bottom, top.* Accelerator experiments, including those at SLAC and Fermilab, have given evidence of all six flavors. And now—for every quark flavor there is an *anti-quark*.

Antiparticles are a mystery in our universe. Every particle has an antiparticle, not just the quark. They exist but we see them so rarely and why? In particle physics, antimatter is composed of antiparticles, which have the same mass as particles of ordinary matter but have opposite charge. Encounters between particles and antiparticles lead to annihilation of both, which then releases energy. If an electron encounters a positron they annihilate each other and transform their mass energies into two gamma rays. So energy is always released in any annihilation and transforms to something else. We observe our universe to be composed almost entirely of ordinary matter, rather than a more symmetric combination of matter and antimatter. It is one of physics biggest unsolved conundrums. Cosmic ray studies (as in Carl and MURA's mountain top experiment) have been able to identify *positrons* and *antiprotons*, seemingly produced by high-energy collisions between particles of ordinary matter. Particle accelerators commonly produce anti-particles, which raised the public's concern, but physicists say there is no reason for alarm. They are so few that show up with so brief a life. The antiquark has not taken over the universe or we would be annihilated. Why haven't they taken over? And the 'whys' and 'whats' continue.

Why can't we pin down the solitary quark?

What gives the quark and particles and atoms and matter, for that matter, mass?

Why do the six flavors of quarks each have different masses?

Why is the top quark, 35 times bigger than the bottom quark, so massive compared to the others?

What is the next universe, presuming there is one, made of?

The world of particle physics is as alive as ever. The questions will never end. We want to know from end to end—how far does the universe extend—forever to infinity?—how miniscule can we go?— does the quark still have a part we can take apart?—or is there NO end?

Quark

As Carl and his colleagues went to the top of Mount Evans to hunt for quarks we too can climb the mountain for an epiphany. We're all capable of finding answers to big questions. Put it all together; stack knowledge on top of knowledge like the particle beams are stacked in an accelerator. And like the scientists build on previous knowledge to come up with new theories that become facts, we can reach a critical mass and uncover the answers that are right in front of our searching eyes.

Ethel Erickson Radmer

REJECTION

October 2013

You can forget almost anything in your life
but you don't forget the things that hurt you . . .
e e radmer

Rejection is painful. It hurts hard and bad. It can be felt as intensely as physical pain. In fact rejection registers in the brain in the dorsal anterior cingulate and the anterior insula, according to researchers Naomi Eisenberger at UCLA and Kipling Williams at Purdue, in the same regions that are activated with physical pain. When you are rejected you feel pain in your brain like you do when you have a punch in the stomach or a stab in the chest, and as severe as the pain of natural childbirth. That's high level discomfort. Psychologists now say that the pain of rejection goes way beyond other powerful emotions, such as fear, in the intensity of discomfort that it manifests. And people don't forget it. It leaves a scar that can last their lifetime. They might forget a lot of good things but the pain of rejection stays in the memory bank, festering. I've heard people, years later, saying that someone rejected them and they remember every detail. It is very hard to let go. A friend of mine remembered my telling him on the phone to not call so much. Years later he reminded me of that incident. The best I could do was say I was sorry.

Rejection packs a wallop of strong attendant feelings. There is a cascade of emotions that surfaces in the blink of an eye when someone sees and feels that they have been rejected. The mountain surges out of a mole hill with, literally, intense hot prickles in the skin and a stoppage and cramping of the digestive tract. It feels toxic and is toxic to our emotional well-being and to our physical state. Our senses register repudiation, a rebuff, turndown, a cold shoulder and exclusion, a slap in the face and a dampening and nixing of our equilibrium. The emotions show up and pour out as anxiety, depression, envy, resentment, sadness and a sense of loss. That adds up to a spectrum of bad feelings that interfere with our contentment. It all stings. I think that rejection has been a universal issue, very strong in our lives, without our realizing it or even acknowledging it.

And it hurts to realize that for many years, few psychologists gave attention to the importance of rejection. According to Professor Mark Leary at Duke University, the whole field of psychology until the past decade and a half passed up this pervasive part of human life. They realize now that the implications of being excluded, when we innately need to belong, are far-reaching.

It's an evolutionary thing. When humans first showed up on this earth, we needed social groups to survive. So, cooperative societies evolved and people depended on these groups for their lives. A need for acceptance was essential to stay part of the group. Otherwise, if they were cast out, they couldn't really manage on their own to find food, drink and safety. There is the proverbial safety in numbers when meeting up with a wild beast or just crossing the road. The African savannah, which birthed the first upright bipeds with a prefrontal cortex, was too harsh for a loner. Wild animals would eventually outsmart and overpower the one alone.

So today we've retained this need to be accepted and even welcomed to the family of human beings. Even extreme loners feel the sting of being left out or dismissed. Their pain might be even stronger with their lack of social support. Maybe the reason they are loners in the first place is their not wanting the rebuffs and turn-downs of another person in their lives. It hurts too much.

My Qi Gong Master teacher, Shifu Michael Hronas, told my class a couple of years ago "there are three things that cause cancer: abandonment, betrayal and rejection." That's a pretty serious indictment of rejection, if it is true. And abandonment and betrayal smack of rejection, also. I suggest that when we feel the intense emotional pain of rejection it disrupts the balance in our body, depresses immunity and sets us up for disease. Cancer developing would be no surprise. And I think, just as we took the pain on, we can reject it (a good rejection!) and overcome the negatives to regain peace for our psyche and balance in our body.

What forms in real-life dramas does rejection take?

Being turned down for a job, having a manuscript sent back, getting the thin envelope with a rejection letter for the college you most wanted to attend, being picked last for the neighborhood kids' sandlot softball team, not being invited to social events, family members not wanting anything to do with other family members and feeling the loss of someone who doesn't want to see you anymore. And then there's the romantic partner rejection—they say no to a date, they don't show up, they leave you bereft and alone without another word from them, they divorce you and leave you with responsibilities you can hardly manage. It all hurts.

I have not been invited to at least a dozen weddings of good friends whom I thought would surely want me there. I waited until enough time had passed, only to learn that an acquaintance was attending. I wondered why I wasn't invited and I felt left out.

I make phone calls to far-away and close-by friends to stay in touch and, except for a few who reciprocate regularly, it's all in my hands. We have good conversations and they are animated with the attention and sometimes show appreciation but they never take a turn at calling me. I rise above the disappointment of the 'rejection' and reach out again because I want us to maintain the connection—life doesn't last forever. And I've never regretted keeping the line open.

For everyone rejected there has to be a person who does the rejecting. And in the spirit of confession, I admit to deliberately and openly rejecting at least one person in my life. Several years ago, a new friend came on too strong for me with a host of ideas for further times together and friends that I must meet. A week later, I called her on the phone and told her that I was sorry but a friendship with her just didn't fit in my life and I wanted to tell her now. She wondered what she had done or said and I put the blame on me—there just wasn't space or time for my being a friend to her. For myself I needed to not take a chance on further overtures. Ever since, I've felt great relief with having done that, with no regrets. I needed the assurance of an end for my own peace of mind. Which gives one example of what might be on the rejecters' mind. My friend probably felt pain with that and may still wonder why. But I couldn't keep it up with her and be content. And there are probably people who feel rejected with a word or even a look or lack of it from me, without my knowing. It's easy to hurt people's feelings without intending to and we do know how it feels in turn.

When I was young and I was going to my neighbor's house to see if my friend, Audrey could play with me, my mother told me "They might not want you there," That stayed with me. It might seem a harsh thing to say from a mother, whose kindness and caring was the core of her being, but it was honest of her. It was a revelation to me that people might not want me and I felt a little badly, but I seemed to realize from the way my mother said it that it was not necessarily a bad thing; just a fact of life. I think that helped to blunt the sting of further rebuts. I didn't take it so personally. Mother did me a favor. Since then I've always been sensitive to other people's perceptions of rejection. I know it can hurt and so I've worked hard to avoid making others feel rejected.

It's not just friends or acquaintances that might reject us. Family members do too. Witness the thousands of aging parents put into nursing homes instead of being taken care of at home as families used to do and in some other countries still do. Granted some do need the medical care of an institution and many families are not able to take care of an aging relative. But they must feel rejected, particularly if they are losing a little of their capacity to manage all the things in their life with changes in hearing, sight, balance and memory. The new, strange surroundings of a retirement home must be very disorientating, compounding their challenges and perhaps hastening their demise. A family today finds it easier than in the past to farm out their loved one because our culture approves and encourages the growth of retirement communities and the attendant assisted living facilities. But I've heard from some medical professionals that there is a trend today toward providing more care at home. Private health groups are offering different levels of assistance to help keep the person in their own home or apartment that they know and are used to. Rejection is then kept at bay.

And here's another sensitive topic. I've heard of adoptees, with wonderful adoptive families, happy throughout their years and then, later in life, making inquiries of their biological parents. Only to find out that their biological parents later married and had children whom they kept and raised. And the biological parents didn't necessarily want to reconnect with their given-up child. That left the child bereft that they were the one not wanted, given up by their parents, even though it was all for good reason, It was a huge blow to them and they were devastated. They had been rejected. Now they were left with an enormous challenge to recover their balance.

The pain of all rejection registers on a variable scale, depending on your investment in the outcome, how vulnerable you are to some situations, how strong you are to bounce back, what kind of social support you have to get you through and what strategies you make up or discover that help you to rise above the discomfort.

Talking it over with a friend or family member might be good for you if you find an agreeable person but it isn't necessarily the best thing to do. I have seen and read many personal growth authors and mentors recommend such a thing—"Find a good listener who won't judge you, won't impose their own stories on you and will understand your pain." Well, in my view, that's expecting a lot. It can be an imposition on someone else to hear you out. What if you can't find that person who will listen without judging or wanting to tell their own story? And I also think the personal growth writers and leaders are modifying their responsibility for their advice by their suggesting you should find a friend to listen. And with all the talk of finding someone to talk to, is it less of a good thing to *not* have someone to talk to? There are always counselors with different letters after their names to go to and they might be a great help to you. But maybe they're not good for you (there are NO sacred cows with me!) and you choose not to go to them for whatever your reason. Maybe the best thing is to explore yourself and find your own answers to your pain.

Besides the pain of feeling pain, here's a motivating factor to do something proactive and not just wallow in emotional disturbance. Realize that someone who shows their hurt on being rejected is not very attractive to others. If you are an unhappy presence because your friend or family member rejected you, they are less likely to want to be with you. Your responding to rejection by revealing your damaged heart can be counterproductive. You want solace and acceptance but you are more likely to be rejected again. This reality can be a reason to dig deeper in your own psyche and do something about it inside yourself.

So what do we do about this bad feeling? We shouldn't have to saddle ourselves with it. It gets in the way of peace of mind and being fully engaged.

In my own journey of personal growth I have come up with truisms and strategies to ease the pain, anxiety and distress of rejection. Here are some of my truisms to confront and to come to terms with in alleviating your discomfort:

ETHEL'S TRUISMS

- You cannot control everything that happens in your life.
- You cannot write the script for someone else.
- You cannot change people. It's not within our power. You can make attempts to let them know what you want and don't want. But in the end, it's their call. And how much energy do you want to expend to try to change things, particularly if you're on edge with constantly monitoring and evaluating developments?
- There is always going to be something you want to change. You might have brief satisfaction and then you just go to the next thing. You can't make the perfect world for yourself by enlisting others to change themselves.
- You cannot tell people what to do or not to do. There is a natural tendency on the part of others to resist such requests. They are in control of their own lives, just like you are in control of yours. Take people as they are and appreciate all the good.
- Something inside of us can have a problem with most anything. The solution to our problem is not to rearrange things outside.

There will always be things to make different. Confront the inner self and change is possible.

- We all have pain in our lives—the amount and frequency vary.
- We all experience rejection and we know that it is possible to bounce back.
- Rejection is in the eye of the beholder.
- The rejecter may not recognize his or her actions as rejection.
- It is possible to not have any bad feelings when someone rejects you.

Ralph Waldo Emerson says, "For everything that you have missed, you have gained something else, and for everything you gain, you missed something else." Looking at life that way gives us some perspective on anything and everything.

In the face of rejection, we can work on us. That means facing up to those social realities in the crux of rejections. That helps. But to be even more proactive in mollifying a wide range of emotions attendant to rejection, here are some suggestions from my own experience. And know that there could be multiple, overlapping ways to solve this problem. It's up to you.

ETHEL'S STRATEGIES:
- Observe what you are feeling.
- Feel the energy of the pain.
- Cry if you feel like it.
- Reshape the pain. Such as if you could somehow see the rebuke as an opportunity.
- Deflect any barbs that you haven't yet recreated, with good, sincerely kind comments to the rejecter, such as "You could look at it that way" or "I understand" or "I'll miss our times together" or "May the journey be good for both of us." And if you are

unable or choose not to speak directly to the person, think and say it to yourself.

- Experience rejection as something else. Don't see it as rejection but as just a fact of life, as an expression of the other person's own agenda which you do not know.
- Realize that the person doing the rejecting is in their way doing the best they can in the interest of protecting their own human fragility.
- Relate to people openly without fear of rejection.
- See it as an opportunity to move on to other people or plans.
- When bad things happen make good of it.
- Do something special for you, like make a day trip to a nature haven—the beach, a park walking trail, a mountain climb. Or hang out in an arboretum or in city gardens, find a bench and read. Nature restores.
- Plan something else like going to a movie or a concert instead of the event you were not invited to. Going alone can be the best thing—make it so!
- Be playful in a myriad of ways.
- Play it as a game. 'You're rejected' is the reality. Replay and redo it in your mind by repeating the rejection out loud in a variety of ways and in a range of dramatic voices to obliterate the bad feeling.
- Learn a lesson from it.
- Take it seriously with no remorse, angst, upset, sadness, anxiety or defensiveness.
- Get out of the fray. In whatever form that takes—moving, leaving, changing your job, creating a new paradigm,
- Actively seek a new partner or friend or confidant in your life.

- Tell someone that they are a wonderful person.
- Feel grateful for one thing and let the list grow longer through the days and decades.
- Delight in a new adventure.
- Have someone tell you that you matter.
- If a romantic partner or friend doesn't want you; think "if they don't want me I don't want them." It's not revenge. It's a practical consideration. Don't waste time with this. Move on. Think "I'm in such a good place."
- Know that you are in a perfect place at all times and are experiencing the present moment with love and acceptance.
- Send love and good thoughts to all.

Welcome to the world of acceptance. Where we all are doing the best we can in our own way. We all have choices to make. We all matter. Instead of a rebuff you are welcomed. Obliteration is replaced with ratification. Instead of illegitimacy you are sanctioned. There is no renunciation, only conciliation. Approval trumps disapproval. Rejection takes a back seat to invitation.

We are wiser now and make choices to be happy within. Instead of being turned down we are turned up to see and experience a braver world. Each one of us is courageous enough to embrace kindness. There is warmth enough to light the passions of the goodness within us. And it expands and grows until we are infused with good will that brightens the world. What a better place we are in!

SPINOZA

March 2014

I'm revisiting Spinoza after six decades of absence since college. Yes! It has been that long! A lifetime goes by in a flash of a meteor, in the streak of a falling star. It is enough (or maybe never enough) to make one philosophical. To become reflective and erudite to pursue deep, learned, rational and even profound thought. With a lifetime, however long, chalked up, we can all be philosophers. Everyone is capable of this and of letting the urges to ponder rise to the surface. And you can let any noted philosopher, who has thoughts recorded in some fashion, be your guide for you to agree or disagree, it matters not. You just want to stir your brain to work on those big questions in life. So, for me, Spinoza has returned, as the talisman of what he calls truth. Though, I admit that his school of thought as well as that of many other learned philosophers, has been part of my thinking almost daily. As in Zafon's 2001 novel, *The Shadow of the Wind*, where Spinoza's *Tractatus Theologico-Politicus* sits side by side with Moratin's plays and a brand-new *Curial e Guelfa* on the bookstore shelf in Barcelona, so too my *Spinoza* writings stood for decades of a peripatetic life on a variety of shelves, butted up against my college paper, *Johnathan Edwards' Doctrine On The Freedom Of The Will*, and a plethora of books and authors I had read.

When I left my small home town in Wisconsin for college to the big city of Chicago, I was primed for study. Both my parents had been a huge influence on me for many things and one of the things was philosophy. My mother, the very religious one, dispensed her Biblical ethical concerns to us kids almost daily. My father used reason, was a strong believer in practicing rational thinking and he wrote and talked his free thinking philosophy, with stacks of books to reference.

The college offerings were a wide range of subjects to sign up for and true to form I wanted to take everything! Biology, English, Literature, History, Psychology and more made for a heavy load. But happily, Professor Lindahl's 'Philosophy and Ethics' class fit right in to my first year's schedule. That is where I wrote a 15 text-page paper, *The Ethics of Spinoza* with a bibliography from the late 1800's to the early 1900's. Fast forward many years and I took the bound copy off the shelf to have a reread. That led to my rereading Spinoza's own writing including his best known *Ethics*, as well as books by others on Spinoza's philosophy and to my further researching his life. Here was a deep thinker like my dad who presented a clear geometric system that made rational sense. Spinoza was a man of reason, dealing with ethics and morality and God, but he seemed to go beyond and astray from the confines of my Baptist interpretation of the teachings of the Bible. And I think that is why I, as a freshman in college, chose then to write about Spinoza. He was a fresh critical thinker whose postulates opened up a wide world of many possibilities of belief and a chance to discard old ideas that I heartedly welcomed.

Benedict De Spinoza, called Baruch Spinoza early in his life, had his own background to influence his own world of thought. What you were and are becoming make you what you are today. He was born in 1632 to Portuguese-Jewish parents in Amsterdam.

His mother died when he was 6 and his father when he was 22. Barush lived his short lifetime of 44 years, dying in 1677 of a lung ailment (possibly tuberculosis or silicosis from the fine glass dust inhaled while grinding optical lenses), as a Dutch citizen, moving to other cities within what we now call the Netherlands and in his last years he moved to The Hague. His birth family members were forced converts to Christianity (called Judaizing Marranos) but living secretly as Jews. His forbears had moved from place to place to avoid persecution as Jews and they still had a 'cross to bear' in Amsterdam. As a member of the synagogue and running his father's merchant business with his brother he was well respected until he began to express his developing unorthodox and heterodox views on religion, philosophy and politics and he gained a reputation as a freethinker (as my dad was also called; his heretical beliefs criticized and he was written off to hell by all the churches in town). Probably to affirm the religious unity of their community the rabbis excommunicated Spinoza which meant that he was banished from all Jewish community life. He eventually moved and took up optical lens grinding and he had an excellent reputation for being very skillful at grinding lenses for microscopes and telescopes that he also made. He could then provide for his needs and at the same time "contemplate things as they really are rather than as we want them to be." He was driving for the naked truth. Which brings us to his philosophical beliefs that were well thought out and formulated as the Spinozean system or school of thought.

Spinoza was strongly influenced by Jewish medieval philosophy and by Descartes, Hobbes and other philosophers who preceded him in life but left their writings behind. He agreed with some of the other philosophers' concepts, disagreed with other ideas and developed his own to fill two books published in his lifetime. A third book, *Opera Postuma* that contained the famous *Ethics*, he did not publish for fear of even more rebuke and his friends published it after his death. Spinoza, in turn, influenced generations of philosophers to come including Hegel (who said you're either a Spinozist or not a philosopher at all) and Deleuze (who called Spinoza the prince of philosophers). Spinoza earned the respect of a few freethinkers like Bayle, Edelmann, Goethe, Shelley, and Byron, who all proposed to translate the *Ethics* jointly after his death.

Quoting from my own paper, "The ethics of Spinoza are unique in that they are presented in geometric form; he offers propositions and proofs for those propositions. Spinoza searched for a method by which all uncertainty could be eliminated and real truth attained. With geometry as a guide, he found it necessary to find axioms such that the number of planets around the sun and the rules for daily living as well could all be deduced just as the theorems of Euclid." In Spinoza's mind all existent things must come from this axiom, again from my paper: "The only adequate source of all things is God. So the basic axiom of Spinoza's system is that God exists. Spinoza defines God as 'a being absolutely infinite, that is a substance consisting in infinite attributes.' God is a thinking thing and an extended thing; God is the only substance there is. This theory is called pantheism. God determines events, not in the sense that a supreme being might voluntarily determine the theorems which follow. Man is not an exception to the universal mechanism, but mind and body are the same thing because they are derived from the same original axioms."

Pantheism was one of the new (for me) concepts in philosophy that expanded my own thinking. It is the belief that the universe or nature is the totality of everything and is identical with divinity. The 'everything' includes an all-encompassing immanence, or I would say a 'nature-based' belief in divinity. This appealed to me because it meant that gods of all different beliefs and creeds were part of the whole.

"How can such a system give help to one who wants to live well?" I asked. "What kind of ethics can be developed from pantheistic predeterminism?"

The ethics that can come from all this is what Spinoza pondered throughout his short life and that he wrote about, as I said in my paper, "The aim of life is to understand each thing in its relation to the whole universe, to follow its deduction from the original axiom, and to see it as an indispensable part of the system, predeterminism."

Spinoza carried on in the same written manner with many philosophical issues that confront us today. And he did it with a formal structure that he devised, including axioms, propositions and proofs, all clear and neat and straight-forward as in a chart. If there ever was a philosopher in my estimation that you could make sense of and understand, Spinoza was the one.

Here is a small sampling of his 'truths' in his own words in the form of his *axioms, propositions* and *proofs*, from his *Ethics*. In them he dealt with God, the nature and origin of the mind and of the emotions and the strength of the emotions.

Axiom VI "By God (*Deus*) I understand a being absolutely infinite, that is, a substance consisting of infinite attributes, each of which expresses eternal and infinite essence." The basic *axiom* (starting point of reasoning) of Spinoza's system is that God exists. And Spinoza defines God as "a being absolutely infinite, that is a substance consisting in infinite attributes."

Axiom IV: "The knowledge of an effect depends on and involves the knowledge of a cause."

Axiom II (Part II): "Man thinks."

With my thinking brain I'll define Spinoza's Propositions as "a statement of his truth." Here are a few.

Proposition XXVIII: "We endeavor to bring about whatsoever we concede to conduce to pleasure; but we endeavor to remove or destroy whatsoever we conceive to be truly repugnant there to, or to conduce to pain."

Proposition VIII (Part IV): "The knowledge of good and evil is nothing else but the emotions of pleasure or pain in so far as we are conscious thereof."

Proposition XIX: "Every man, by the laws of his nature, necessarily desires or shrinks from that which he deems to be good or bad."

Proposition XL: "Whatever conduces to man's social life, or causes men to live together in harmony is useful, whereas whatsoever brings discord into a state is bad."

Proposition XLVII: "Emotions of hope and fear can not be in themselves good."

Proposition LXIII: "He who is led by fear, and does good in order to escape evil, is not led by reason." Spinoza calls us to live by the guidance of reason.

For each of his propositions he gives a proof. It can be succinct as in Proof for Proposition II in Part II: "The proof of this proposition is similar to that of the last." Or the proof can be lengthy to a page. All are written for any eager reader's comprehension.

He expanded on these to say that "part of my happiness is to lend a helping hand." "Understand as much of nature as leads to a good character." "Seek for means which will bring him to this pitch of perfection and calls everything which will serve as such means a true good." "I wish to direct all sciences to one end and aim, so that we may attain to the supreme human perfection which we have named; and, therefore, whatsoever in the sciences does not serve to promote our object will have to be rejected as useless. To sum up the matter in a word, all our actions and thoughts must be directed to this one end." Living an ethical life was of great importance to him and exploring all the philosophical facets of a life well lived he passed on to future generations.

Ethel Erickson Radmer

Much could be made of his axioms, propositions and proofs and philosophers through the ages have mined the territory endlessly. But our knowing can lead to a better understanding of how we live our lives and it can be useful in making the most of what time we have on this earth. And new ways of looking at things can evolve to even more expansive ideas and beliefs.

Just as the metaphysical crowd, psychologists and every other profession, as well as the rest of the human race are searching and caring about finding happiness, seeing a purpose to their lives, wanting answers to big questions and seeking contentment in the midst of turmoil, our new old friend, Benedict De Spinoza explored it, giving today's searchers a heads-up and a head-start on their own thinking and acting, from almost 400 years ago!

His name is still prominent in philosophy studies. He holds court in philosophy discussion groups across the country and probably around the world. Your God, Spinoza, has bestowed blessings on all of us and enriched our lives. God which you say "can only be one," including you and me, is "a being absolutely infinite" and "existence of this kind is conceived as an eternal truth." Your truths live on.

You readers can find his gravesite, with 'Benedict De Spinoza' carved in stone, in the churchyard of the Nieuwe Kerk in The Hague. Rest in peace famous philosopher. By your own words, you will "never cease to be."

Ethel Erickson Radmer

TREE

November 2014

An Ojibwe Indian drum roll, please, in praise of the TREE.

My Land of Hiawatha setting is spacious and spectacular. Snow is falling in November on a seventy foot tall community of white spruce and Colorado Blue tip spruce, just outside the bay window of my hostess's dome home. Waters of the Chain of Lakes surround her point of land on this gray day, as I sit inside and write. I'm warm as a black bear's heart beating in a four hundred pound body, roaming for hickory nuts, grass and berries as his store for the winter's hibernation right in our neighborhood of trees. I heard a bear yesterday, I'm pretty certain, off in the woods, as I took my early morning walk on the dirt road covered with snow. The sound had that low, big snort of a creature alert for threats, when he was the one that could be a danger to me. This strong, smart, mostly vegetarian creature, who will attack when he is provoked, is only one of thousands of life forms, animal and plant that live among trees. They are dependent on, have a symbiotic relations with and a reliance on trees for safety and survival.

The Wisconsin Northwoods stretches up to the edges of Lake Superior, the largest body of freshwater in the world. and occupies a space approximately 120,000 square miles. Thousands of years ago the trees were part of a vast expanse of forested wilderness throughout Europe, Russia, Alaska, Canada and the northern United States, part of which has been lost. The more temperate zones and the tropics on our planet have their rain forests and jungles with the tips of a dense growth of trees reaching for the sun far above the crowded, forest floor. Their existence is in contrast to the deserts in Southern climes, the open Savannah in Africa and the almost treeless expanse of the Australian outback. South America's huge Amazon Forest is teeming with life. Perhaps most importantly to keep other life forms alive is their growth of trees. Midst the ice covered oceans of our polar extremes, north and south, coniferous forests of spruce and pine, with heavily snow laden boughs, grow on frozen land. I've seen noble stands of them in the Arctic Circle. Life adapts to flourish in the coldest of cold. Further north to the Arctic's North Pole there is only tundra and the Arctic Ocean.

It's cold here, too, in the Northwoods but nothing approaching the Poles dropping to 80 degrees below zero Fahrenheit. The forest I walk in or drive through includes a tree variety of sugar maple, red maple, basswood, beach, red oak, white ash, aspen, hemlock, yellow birch and not least, though they have dwindled in numbers from their glory days of the long past, the majestic white pine. With some irony it symbolizes immortality because it is evergreen. But the good news is that many are surviving and are the stronger for it. The white pine may be immortal after all! Enhancing the tree tableau are bushes, mosses, mushrooms, lichens, ferns, berries and wild flowers that fill the forest floor.

To herald diversity, nature has evolved 23,000 kinds of trees in the world, climbing up to 300 feet. There are cacao and plumeria trees, both growing in the heat of South America and of Hawaii, Siberian pine in the Ural Mountains' bitter cold and an emerging array in between. Some are of age beyond belief: the giant sequoia live to 2500 years and the Bristlecone pine last twice as long to

5000 years. Two botanical groupings of all trees include deciduous trees with broad leaves and conifers or evergreens with needles. The names alone give fun and intrigue. Conifers such as cowtail pine or plum yew, alligator juniper, Cedars of Lebanon, monkey puzzle tree and weeping giant sequoia. Broad leafed trees such as full moon maple, cucumber tree, windmill palm, quaking aspen, Carolina silverbell, goldenrain and tree-of-heaven

Their beauty to please all the senses is what captures you. Tall, elegant, short, assertive with thorns as in the acacia tree, wispy but strong as the willow, rich aromas of sassafras leaves, sap and flowers (almost all trees have flowers), tasty fruits with a slogan to encourage adventure—"don't be afraid to go out on a limb … that's where the fruit is." The color range of greens and browns defy your perception. But artists through the ages: music, visual and literary, have tried to capture it.

We have Claude Monet's series of twenty four paintings, all done in 1891, *The Poplars,* an ode to the magnificent poplar tree of freedom and fertility in France. In Herman Hesse's *Siddhartha* we read about Gautama (circa 500 BC) meditating for forty-nine days under a Bodhi tree on a riverbank in India and gaining enlightenment. In the 1940's the Glen Miller Orchestra and the Andrews Sisters made famous "Don't Sit Under the Apple Tree With Anyone Else but Me" during World War II.

Frederic Delarue, a recording artist on the keyboard and an author, said that he asks a tree for permission before he touches or hugs or takes a picture of the tree to use on an album. And he is answered "yes" with a gentle breeze. That's a beautiful, reverential gesture and I would hope the rest of us are sensitive to Nature when we help ourselves to all that the trees have to offer. And give they do. Let me list the ways to remind you:

- Make a beautiful landscape wherever we may dwell.
- Keep our waters clean by soaking up pollutants and sediments.
- Reduce crime (no kidding!) as measured by University of Washington Seattle researchers in outdoor areas planted with trees.
- Give a home to 80 species of wildlife, with higher numbers in the rainforests.
- Make fuel to provide heat
- Serve as a windbreaker in the cold.
- Provide a canopy of shade in the heat and save on AC energy (where are the rows of trees in parking lots to cool hot cars?).
- Give fruits, seeds and nuts for our nourishment.
- Offer spices like cinnamon from the bark of the cinnamon tree and maple syrup from the sap of the sugar maple tree.
- Provide timber from the sturdy trunk for building dwellings, furniture and posts and poles.
- Give us tea tree leaves to make soap, natural latex to make rubber and pine resin to make turpentine.
- Give up the bark from the cork trees in Portugal and other Mediterranean countries to make bottle stoppers and to carve a cork rotary valve bumper for my son-in-law's, my grandson's and my own (long-ago) French horns. A cork rotary stop makes for less noise and the right amount of bounce. And have you walked on cork floor tiles that have that buoyant give to the feet?
- Grow spruce and maple to make musical string instruments including the violin, viola and cello and add birch, poplar, pine, walnut and mahogany for the piano.
- Present tree parts made into pulp and voila the incredible, vital, 'however would we get along without it' paper materializes which I am writing on right now! Words formed, sentences put together on a yellow pad and sheets that add up to books and also cardboard boxes to pack them in—a gift of the phenomenal tree.

Ethel Erickson Radmer

- Make medicine—pharmaceutical, herbal, homeopathic and naturopathic that provide relief and cures and fill thousands of books.
- Offer more uses than you can count or know or maybe use.
- And one more.

May we please hear a Chippewa Indian Powwow drum roll (of hickory, cedar and hide) for the #1 gift of the trees?

Oxygen!

If there were no trees on earth, we humans and other animals would go to our demise. Does that shock you to life?

Trees gather energy from the sun through chlorophyll in their leaves. They use this sun energy to mix with CO_2 and water that contain minerals from the soil. The water is drawn up through xylem in the sapwood of the trunk and on up to the leaves. The sap is the tree's food. In this process called photosynthesis the leaves 'exhale' or give off oxygen into the air. 20% of all the gases in the atmosphere is oxygen. At least half of our oxygen comes from phytoplankton and algae in our oceans and lake water. Water comprises 71% of our earth's surface which leave 29% for land. The rest of our oxygen supply comes mostly from trees. Our population numbers are growing while our forests have receded.

So there it is. We need trees like we need food and water and sleep. We need a resupply of our vital gas oxygen for survival.

All the warnings, accolades, admonitions, quotes, idioms and aphorisms apply:

"Trees are the answer," I saw on the back window of a gold colored Subaru in a Barnes and Noble parking lot.

"The best time to plant a tree is twenty years ago; the second best time in now."

"Who leaves the pine-tree, leaves his friend, unnerves his strength, invites his end." Ralph Waldo Emerson "Woodnotes"

"I like trees because they seem more resigned to the way they have to live than other things do." Willa Cather "O Pioneers" 1913

"Suburbia is where the developer bulldozes out the trees, then names the streets after them." William E. Vaughn

"Climb a tree—it gets you closer to heaven." Anonymous

"The creation of a thousand forests is in one acorn." Ralph Waldo Emerson

"Other holidays repose on the past. Arbor Day proposes the future." J. Sterling Morton

And my own:

"Love a tree and all your cares fall away like autumn leaves drop from their branches." e e radmer

Or, if humans move on to another planet, with the death of our own, we, like Kuno in E. M. Forster's "The Machine Stops" © 1909, "would have yearned for trees to climb."

Trees, please stay alive and multiply. We need you. We love you. We'll do our best to treat you well. Thank you for your heart and for your bark. We wrap our arms around you in one big group hug along our walking paths, across the state and country and around the world. We are in awe of your resilience, your longevity and your grandeur. May you reach for the sky long, long after our generation is gone and the next and the next are outlived by you.

Gratefully yours,
e e radmer
On behalf of People of the World

Ethel Erickson Radmer

UFO and UNIVERSE

September 2014

It started in a time and place I hadn't remembered (and learned much later)—this fascination I have had with UFOs for most of my life. We called them flying saucers when I was a kid and by the time I finished high school in 1953 the US Air Force came up with a more inclusive acronym called UFO or unidentified flying object. They recorded this officially in their Project Blue Book that pretty much debunked any reports they had received from witnesses to objects in the sky or on the ground that the witness could not identify as being of our planet. The official, non-scientific pronouncement (there are no studies and saying it is a balloon needs some support) was that those reported objects were unknown or were aircraft, balloons, clouds, planets, meteors or hoaxes and more recently satellites (which can be tracked on a smart phone). Their conclusions did not seem substantiated or justified to my common sense mind. Where was the science behind those conclusions?

My dad believed these flying saucers could well be coming from outer space and were operated in some fashion by other worldly intelligent life and were indeed appearing in our sky. To me it was logical that balloons or clouds couldn't explain it and I gave credence to people's eyewitness accounts. My dad's open-mindedness, as well as critical thinking, made for fertile ground for my own inquiries and curiosity, which have increased over time.

Way back then our family members, at least silently, asked the big cosmic questions. The Baptists, Methodists, Lutherans and Assembly of God church, all of which our ecumenical family attended, had answers to most questions but they seemed inadequate to the profoundness of my wondering. What is the universe? Is it finite or infinite? If the universe had a beginning how will it end? What is space? Is there intelligent life in outer space? Are those beings from other planets, that must be out there by the laws of chance, trying to contact us? Are we missing the messages? And the most intriguing question for me was, Are we alone?

The Bible, as interpreted by our Protestant clergy, seemed to say we live in one finite universe, the world will end, people will go to either heaven or hell (unknown location in the cosmos), depending on their beliefs about God and Jesus. And we are alone. So, I asked the minister if there are other universes. I asked it with my own conception stretched and by way of saying maybe that is where other beings and worlds could reside. His response was a shocked no and he wondered how I could even think such a thing that was not in God's Word. But my strong curiosity easily overcame that rebuff!

Thoughts of other life forms different from our own earthly variety and of ways for an intelligent being to transport throughout the universe captured and filled the imagination. But, we have an ever-growing map of what makes up our universe that we need to know and there are laws of physics that we operate by in this universe for us to acknowledge and maybe understand in order for us to be sensible about the possibilities of life and searching for those elusive UFOs. May we call them spaceships?

Let me set the stage for exploring the possibilities of extraterrestrial life and of intergalactic and interstellar travel with an overview of the cosmos and as my dad would say, "Facts. Here are the facts." We'll start with the earth, then expand to the solar system, spread to the Milky Way Galaxy and move to and through the entire universe that we can see, with the aid of optics, and possibly other universes with their own laws of physics and mathematics which we do not presently see and can't measure unless we do see. Or possibly there are no other universes. All matter, including heavenly bodies in the universe, has weight and dimension. Size does matter. They also have scale in relation to each other. Figuring out and knowing both dimension and scale is necessary to make the map. Methods and mathematics used for finding and measuring is another essay!

First I'll give you some dimensions of heavenly bodies and secondly their scale, telling us how one object relates to another in space such as the distance between them. Age matters too but doesn't show up as clearly on the map. And numbers vary and get updated with new data from the Hubble telescope, positioned in orbit above the Earth's atmosphere.

We go from our home planet Earth that has a diameter of 25,000 miles and we add a zero to travel 250,000 miles to the moon. The moon has a diameter of 2000 miles (some of these diameter and distance stats are courtesy of the Harvard-Smithsonian Center for Astrophysics). The sun has a diameter of 875,000 miles and is 93 million miles from the earth. A million Earths would fit inside the Sun. Saturn, as one example of the 9 planets (I can't let go of Pluto!), has a diameter of 75,000 miles and is 120 million miles from the earth at its closest while traveling the oval loop around the sun. I'll skip the weights. And that is just our solar system.

Pleiades, in our Milky Way Galaxy, is an example of an open star cluster, moving up in size from our solar system. Pleiades, also called Seven Sisters, is 60 trillion miles across the cluster of stars and is in the constellation of Taurus. It is 2,400 trillion miles from Earth and is among the nearest star clusters to us and the most obvious to the naked eye in the night. I have noticed in my search for UFOs that several witnesses whom I have heard speak, read or talked with report back from their experiences that they were told through ESP or extrasensory perception that the ETs they encountered came from the Pleiades. Why Pleiades? Maybe, it is because it is the closest star cluster to us, at 2,400 trillion miles? It's a puzzle I haven't figured out but it is intriguing. Pleiades is only one of 20,000 open star clusters in the Milky Way. One quarter of these star clusters are invaders from other galaxies (chance of passing on life?), born elsewhere and migrated to the Milky Way over the last couple of billion years. About 160 globular star clusters are found just outside our galaxy. They orbit the halo or bulge in the center of our galaxy, in highly elliptical orbits, which take them far outside the Milky Way.

We have creatively put stars together (even though they may be very distant from each other) as we see them in the sky in a formation we call a constellation or a grouping of stars that reside in our Milky Way Galaxy. They are a point of reference (like the map) for learning names of stars and they are used in astronomy as well as astrology. There are 88 (keys on the piano) constellations. Some were grouped and named before the beginning of recorded history and as far back as 4000 BC. They are all over the map and give us even more perspective on our universe. All the visible stars in our sky, except for our Sun, are in these imaginary constellations.

We move on from star clusters and constellations to the whole disc-shaped Milky Way Galaxy, measuring 600,000 trillion miles across. Even though we are inside the galaxy the distance can be somehow measured and pictures have been taken of it from all parts of the earth to reveal a stretched out horizontal, flat-liner landscape in space with a supermassive (the biggest kind) black hole hump in the middle. Remember when the world's inhabitants thought the world was flat?! With my bent for UFOs I would describe our spiral galaxy as looking distinctly flying saucer-like!

Gazing on our Milky Way Galaxy from within, we will do a count. Our solar system with our sun and earth sits about 2/3 of the way from the center to the edge of this spiral galaxy. Milky Way holds hundreds of billions of stars. Each star probably has a planetary system with at least one planet. All planets outside of our solar system orbiting a star other than our sun are called exoplanets. So far astronomers have (for real) discovered over 1,800 exoplanets, as of this month of my writing, September 2014, and estimate there could be 400 billion exoplanets. Considered separately, scientists say that there are a trillion or more lone planets free floating in the galaxy without a sun to revolve around. An anomaly of a trillion!

And as a final distance stat, if we stretch out further through space, beyond the Milky Way to the entire scope of many billions of galaxies that can be seen with the Hubble telescope, their distance is 30 sextillion miles from Earth. All of the galaxies that the Hubble telescope sees measure 600 quintillion miles across the cluster of galaxies. And to top off those growing numbers scientists say that this is an expanding universe by almost all calculations! The picture is getting bigger and bigger!

If you want to take those mile measurements and translate them to light-year units of length, know that one light-year is equal to 5.88 trillion miles and you can do the math. A light-year is defined as the distance that light travels in vacuum in one year. The speed of light is 186,000 miles per second. It travels at 671 million miles per hour. At the speed of light you could go around Earth 7.5 times in one second. To measure great distances, astronomers use light years as well as the parsec or pc which is about 3.26 light-years.

Our big hunt for life is on for a sun-like star with an earth-like planet that is not gas and is in the habitable zone—that is with sufficient atmospheric pressure to have liquid water and is in a middle planet position on the spiral to not get too much or too little radiant energy from a star or sun. The number of those possibly habitable planets discovered is increasing almost daily to hundreds and estimates are between 11 billion potentially habitable earths on up to 40 billion. There are a lot of ways to categorize, exclude, include and to do the counting. The nearest planet to us in that Goldilocks Zone is expected (not quite discovered) to be within 12 light-years distance from the Earth. Throw those numbers into the odds of there being intelligent life somewhere else than earth.

Age is another consideration in our awareness of the world around us and for imagining life in other places. But there is a catch to age. What you are seeing in a telescope of a star in our galaxy or in another galaxy is already long, long ago history because of the time that image takes to get to you. In present time that star image may have changed from a red giant to a white dwarf or exploded into a supernova and we don't know it. What an intelligent being on a planet in Pleaides is seeing on Earth in their 'now' is long ago history on our planet. We need to know age to compare and to see our relationship to other heavenly bodies. Earth is 4.5 billion years old, as is our moon, Saturn, all our other planets and the sun. Pleiades is 80 million years old but the whole Milky Way Galaxy is 10 billion years of age. And all the other galaxies that the Hubble telescope takes in are also 10 billion years old. What is beyond those galaxies could be even more galaxies and universes that astronomers think exist. Perhaps it is just space but where does it end or not end? Is it an infinite universe with no age at all?

Well, that boggles the mind. How do you wrap your head around an infinite universe? Everything we know is finite. Our thinking is finite. All the measuring we just did is inherently finite. And time is bent because of distance, which almost warps my thinking!

We have set the stage and it's a big one. We exist in at least three dimensions and perhaps a lot more according to physicists. We have a lot of information and know where some of the unknowns are. There are puzzles and questions and wonderings. So with experiences and speculation, I'll go back to where I began—my fascination with UFOs.

Are there UFOs and ETs out there in this grand universe who visit us on Earth? I think there are. I have looked for decades, read shelves of books, met many people in my everyday life by chance who have seen UFOs and sometimes ETs. Like attracts like? I have family members who have seen spaceships when they were kids, teenagers and adults, in the air, on the ground and coming out of the ocean. I've gone to conferences on UFOs and heard speakers with amazing stories. You can read the books. I've joined groups including Dr. Steven Greer, who has weeklong training sessions coast to coast, to learn how to make contact with ETs. I've done remote viewing that is useful in seeing what's out there. I have made special trips with my husband who, when he was alive, was just as fascinated or more so as me in spaceships and extraterrestrial beings. On one of our ventures at two in the morning he spontaneously climbed the high, steel mesh fence to a cemetery in upstate New York that a UFO book author acquaintance of mine often visited to see huge triangular craft with lights hanging low in the sky and zipping away at incredible speeds. I have searched out crop circles in England with a helicopter and pilot and gave a talk on the subject to a museum in Massachusetts. About a dozen years ago I visited the country home and acreage in Vermont of a friend who saw a spaceship with lights in the early evening hover over the grass in her yard several years earlier. She showed me where the ship had left a large ring of yellow grass in the middle of the normal green, stopping the growth but not seeming to have killed it. I could see it clearly, even after 4 years. She seemed reluctant to say very much about it, as many witnesses are, so I didn't pepper her with questions, but I wondered if ETs revealed themselves to her or if she had the classic 'missing time' when her memory of an encounter was blocked.

Know these things; that in spite of what you read in books or see in the Hollywood movies, ETs are benevolent. If they were not we wouldn't still be here. If ETs are able to make it here in spaceships from wherever and however in the galaxies and over many light years of distance, their technology is far superior to ours and their social mores and behavior are advanced to a level way beyond our warmongering ways. Or we would all be annihilated. They leave us to our own devices but they have saved us on occasion, such as in making inoperable or taking 'off alert' our nuclear missiles at the Minot Air Force Base in North Dakota in 1967 and at other times and bases, coinciding with the reported presence of craft of unknown origin.

They like the beauty of our Earth, which says to me there is great diversity in the universe. They give us signs, if we are alert, open and aware, like making crop circles of incredible beauty and mathematical complexity (forget the hoaxes), messages sent via extrasensory perception, spaceship lights flashing and speeding beyond what we know, making a dead stop in mid-air and turning on a dime. We don't have aircraft that can do that. They flash lights on the ground that you can't explain in any other way than it must have come from a spaceship, as I saw a big patch of red light, with others at night, on the Gulf of Mexico beach sand in Florida in February 2014.

How do they get here, you ask. The Hubble telescope has fine-tuned the distance to Pleiades at about 440 light-years from earth. So if an ET traveled the speed of light to Earth from Pleiades it would take 440 years to get here. Knowing the incredible distances ETs might travel, it seems impossible by physics laws. But let me open the door a little on the speed of light. Einstein set the speed limit on how fast things can move. His Special Relativity theory has a postulate that says that nothing can travel faster than light. It is the speed at which all particles without mass and electromagnetic radiation (light) and gravitational waves travel in vacuum. And to add to the challenge of getting there or here, it would take an infinite amount of energy as we know it to accelerate an object with mass to the speed of light. The faster you go the heavier you get but you would age very little. Perhaps there are energy sources beyond our present capability. And remember that Special Relativity is a theory and not a law. The Geneva Higgs Boson accelerator picked up data that seemed to show particles traveling at a speed greater than the speed of light but it has not been substantiated. Fifteen billion years ago, the Big Bang expanded matter from nothing in a massive expansion to incredible distances in a fraction of a second. How did that happen? That's certainly faster than the speed of light. There is so much we do not know. There was science in the past that we believed was true and later with more information we learned is blatantly false. With new knowledge comes an expansion of the possibilities of explaining things.

For energy sources to whip your spaceship through space consider electro-magnetic and anti-gravity propulsion systems or find ways to extract energy from the space between atoms known as zero point energy or the quantum vacuum.

To make the trip happen in an instant, try these words on for size: teleportation and dematerialization. Science fiction has often been prescient about technologic advances to come and I think our future will reveal capabilities beyond imagining. A spaceship and an ET on some habitable planet in a star system in Pleiades both dematerialize and then, without traveling, they rematerialize on Earth. Two particles a great distance apart make a connection, interact and pass information—call it quantum entanglement or Bell's theorem. Teleport information to a planet and the ET and its spaceship are reborn. And you may have ideas of your own!

About three years ago when I was doing research for my memoir, *Walking the Rails*, I spent weeks going through my mother's diaries covering many years, a lifetime ago, every page packed with stories and information. Somewhere along the way I read from her 1946 Diary (when I was 10 years old), and a shiver of recognition waved through my body. In my own book I wrote *"On April 29, 1946, while I was out playing at night, I saw a big star that looked nearly as big as the sun. Then it got scattered into several little stars. I told Mom and she recorded it in her diary, but neither one of us read any sign into it that I remember. The moon was a waning crescent at twenty-seven days old. Mercury, Venus and Saturn were in the evening sky but were not in a confluence. My parents kept track of eclipses of the moon and sun for us to watch. I loved looking to the sky for all the years I can remember and would call Mom and Leone out to look at rainbows…Then, seeing the big star get scattered into several little stars in '46 kept me fascinated with the heavens and looking for other mysterious sky happenings ever since."*

So that's where my enchantment with UFOs began.

VITALITY

December 2013

We found ourselves a while back in time, seemingly out of nowhere, planted on this earth and slowly becoming aware of our physical being. A loving body next to us gave sustenance to our urges. Senses came alive to see, hear, feel, taste and smell. Emotions grew. There was comfort in the resting by our mother's breast. The sounds of her softly singing a tune filled us with peace. Being held by others embraced our small forms with love. There was light in our eyes to take this new world into our dawning awareness. It was the genesis of our being alive. The debut of new life unfolded. The embarking on a unique journey of joys and perils had begun.

Let's wrap it all up like a gift to each one of us and use one word to describe this capacity to live, grow and develop. VITALITY. It is *life force* and I feel it every day. Vitality, sourced from Latin, distinguishes us the living from the nonliving or dead. The principle of life, the ability to live and exist, and animation all play out in our very real experiences here and now.

I see numerous words in the English language that are *vitality*'s dictionary neighbors and 'vi' relations. A poi puree of like-minded words include: *vim, vigor, vital, vitalize, vitalization, vitalizer, vibrant, vibrancy, vivify* (to give or bring life to)*, virility*, and *vigorous*. They all have the kernel of the ebullient *vitality*—our power to live. *Vitamin* comes close with organic (live) substances essential for normal growth and activity of the body. And remember Vivian Walker or 'Vivi' in the novel, *Divine Secrets of the Ya-Ya Sisterhood?* She was the leader of the group of women who caused shenanigans and chaos everywhere. They were living life to the hilt in their own way. Her name, *Vivian,* (used for both sexes) originated in Latin from the masculine *Vivianus* and the feminine *Viviana,* Those words are related to the adjective *vivus,* meaning 'lively' and 'alive.' Sidda, daughter to Viva wondered about all the 'v' words in her Webster's dictionary that she said referred to her mama and of which Vivian was the source. *Vivid* was "full of life; bright; intense." *Vivify* was to "to give life or to make more lively." Others words she found were *vivace, viva, vivacious, vivacity, vivarium,* and *viva voce.* "All the definitions had to do with life," Sidda said, "like Mama herself."

Chi or *Qi* is 'vital force' or 'life energy' in Chinese and is spoken of in the well know practices of Chi Gong and Tai Chi, in which I've participated while visiting Beijing. *Prana* is 'life energy' in Hindi. I've heard Deepak Chopra speak in Agra, India about this life energy, or *Prana*, being channeled throughout our bodies by a 'wind' known as *Vata*. Vata gives form to every living thing and is responsible for movement of every kind. The 'life force' may be hard to pin down but the words go on: *Prana Vata, Udana Vata, Samana Vata, Vyana Vata* and *Apana Vata*, all of which regulate our body processes that sustain life.

Businesses, healing arts groups and schools across the county include the word "Vitality" in their names to elevate the importance of their work and attract you to their cause. I'll give my own inclusive, generic titles and variations to the hundreds, maybe thousands of such groups: Academy on Vitality and Aging, Vitality Chiropractic, Vitality College for the Healing Arts, Vitality Oriental Arts, Massage for Vitality and periodicals using Vitality as part of or the whole of their name, Make up your own name and trademark it if you can! But vitality is the property of ALL! It is in everyone's possession. There are no exclusivity rights to such an all-encompassing manifestation of *vitalitet* in Swedish, *vitalidad* in Spanish, *vitaliteit* in Dutch, *vitalidade* in Portuguese, *vitality* in Italian, *vitalityt* in German and *vitality* in French.

The field of medicine defines vitality as the peculiarity of distinguishing living from nonliving and of physical or mental vigor especially when highly developed. They speak of 'vital signs' for life and death and we hear of 'vital statistics' to measure our closeness to the nonliving state.

Expressions that we see include: vitality in writing, economic vitality, intellectual vitality, creative vitality, actors bringing vitality to their work, architecture infused with vitality, vitality of an institution or of a language, sexual vitality and the vitality of a seed to grow. And that's pretty much where we all start—as a seed or zygote that is infused with vitality.

Vitality, I can say, without much equivocation, is the thing we *most* want in life! We all want a healthy capacity for vigorous activity (if we don't want it, perhaps our libido is low and vitality is registering near the bottom on our scale). It goes way beyond just living—to revving up the output! Va-va-voom! It encapsulates the ultimate in vim and vigor. It is the pinnacle of our life force. Some power is making us evolve and grow as an organism. We don't see it, but we can imagine this invisible force at work to fuel evolution, growth and change in an organism, all the way from the simple, single-celled paramecium and ameba to our complex human selves.

Think about vitality's importance. We want to be alive and in top form with all parts working. Good nutrition is a given. There is ebullient vitality and energy present with practices of thoughtful eating and flowing movement. We have balance in all our body processes and in the strenuous use of the muscular system. Our spirit (if its existence is questionable for you, have you heard, "When your spirits are low?"), our mind, and emotions are rising to higher, positive, productive levels. Wherever a life form is positioned on the family tree, there are degrees of vital forces that manifest, as on a spectrum. You can be a sick creature, barely functioning but still alive with your state of vibrancy low. Children might be given a label of 'health impaired' by the medics, when they have limited strength, alertness and vitality with any number of illnesses. And at the other end of the spectrum, you can have life force that is radiating energy and is balanced to the winds. When we are energetic and accomplished, our vitality is noticed and noted. We are squeezing everything out of life. There is no half-way. And there is nothing getting in the way.

Which brings up this: if you have low vitality, what is getting in the way? Well, without even knowing you, I can say there are roadblocks and barriers that need to come down. Ferret out the blocks and make them dissolve. Numerous things are sapping and draining your energy. Find them; acknowledge their presence and what they are doing to you. Have a will to change your patterns and direction. Come to terms with non-nourishing emotions, such as hurt, sadness, anxiety and upset. Let them go. Feel the weight of them lift and experience an incredible lightness of being. It could and should be that way for humanity all of the time. And then vitality in its highest form can exist within each of us to bless every waking moment.

My 28 year-old grandson, a lawyer in Japan, wrote me recently. He told me that, "Everybody here in Japan says you're 'genki'." Genki means lots of things: health(y), robust, vigor, vigour, energy, vitality, vim, stamina, spirit, courage, pep."

My dear grandson, I'll take that with a most grateful heart! I'm *genki* and vitality is part of it. It comes with an extra dose and notice of life.

WYOMING

Chapter 9 from *My Odyssey With Two Uncommon Boys: A Trip To The Western States*
© 2009 Ethel Erickson Radmer

WYOMING WELCOMES YOU, says the state sign. It shows a high mound of rock with gold ridges and a silhouette of a bucking horse and a cowboy. He's hanging on with his right hand, and with his left hand he's holding, with flair, a cowboy hat high in the air. Yee Ha! We're in Wyoming!

The boys look ever so confident and endearing as they lean casually and comfortably against their posts, making short shadows toward me as I take a snapshot of their efflorescing lives.

We are going to Devil's Tower, the rock on that sign, to see a 40 million year old monolith. One of Nathan's college friends, a native of Wyoming, had urged him to see it and so we are.

The elevation of the surrounding prairie is rising to 4,000 feet. We are in a state of grasslands and mountains. Far to the west near the Wyoming-Idaho border, beyond our travel route, is the blue and jagged Grand Teton Mountain Range. Among those mountains, thrusting almost 14,000 feet into the thin, clear air, live the moose and bison. The Rocky Mountains begin there. Just north of the Tetons are two million acres of Yellowstone, home to the black and grizzly bears, and filled with thousands of thermal vents. Deep down to its molten-rock core, the restless earth is rumbling and fuming steam from its fumeroles and bubbling mud pots, to its geysers and natural hot springs. Seeing those geological wonders would mean at least half a day's drive and back again, each way, through the Bighorn Mountains and we don't have time for that this time. And the Oregon Trail, crossing southern Wyoming, is not an option. The Trail served the settlers well—the homesteaders, fur traders and gold prospectors, the Mormons congregating at Salt Lake and the cowboys-to-be—all looking for free land, compliments of the U.S. government and to the detriment of the Indians, in the far west. Then the Union Pacific Railroad was built in Wyoming. It connected westward with the Central Pacific Railroad building eastward. This first transcontinental railroad, stretching from Council Bluffs, Iowa, to Sacramento, California, was completed in 1869. It usurped the need for a wagon and oxcart path. So we three modern day travelers in an 'iron conveyance' stay course on the middle plane.

Directly south of us to the Colorado border, another half day's drive that we will not make, is Cheyenne, population 50,000, the Wyoming capital and the largest city in this sparse state of the fewest people in the country.

"I"ll tell my friend," Nathan says, "that we did not have time to visit the capitol with its real gold leaf dome."

"And as for the Governor," I add, "Democratic Governor Dave Freudenthal, the common man, is listed in the phone book, so we can give him a call if we want to, rather than an attempted visit."

"Maybe I will phone him," Nathan kids. "I may want his permission to prospect for gold. Kenny, you could prospect with me. Mineral extraction, especially coal, is the main industry in Wyoming, but there is still gold to be found."

"I'd like to do that. It suits me. I like to be outdoors, I like to take chances and I might make some money like I hope to do with playing poker," Kenny says enthusiastically. He takes it seriously.

Ethel Erickson Radmer

"Mmmm," I pondered out loud. "The poor man's coal and the rich man's gold. Gambling can incur both. But, if you do plan to dredge, you need a state permit and I wish you luck. One of my brothers, a chemical engineer, prospected for gold and uranium and other minerals for many years in his free time in this very state. What he was left with was thousands of dollars down the drain."

"Or dribbled through the gold sifter," Nathan jokes.

We turn off of 1-90 onto U.S.14, skimming the fringes of Wyoming's Black Hill Country, home to the Black Hills Spruce and ponderosa pine. The Black Hills extend from here back into South Dakota, where we'll visit again later today. Triceratops made these Hills their home 65 million years ago.

Kenny, Nathan and I can see, from miles away, a fluted, flat-topped cone that rises hundreds of feet into the air. Now, stepping out of the van onto its rocky floor, we see the impressive sight up close. Alone in profile against the deep blue sky is another mystery like the Badlands. Where did this come from in the middle of the plains? How do you explain such eerie beauty? The Indians considered this as holy, the site of the ancient Sun Dance, but called it Bad God's Tower. Today it's called Devil's Tower National Monument. It is likely they were trying to frighten off the explorers, but without success. Tribes living in what is now Wyoming—the Shoshones and the Arapahos, the Lakota, Crows, Cheyenne, Bannocks, Blackfoot and Northern Ute—all ranged here centuries ago. Only remnants of tribes have survived. The Europeans, our descendants, arrived in the eastern United States 500 years ago, but it took a while for them to get to Wyoming. John Colter is the earliest known white explorer, because he told stories about it, that were passed on 200 years ago. He was part of the Lewis and Clark expedition, following the Missouri River in Montana. John left the expedition on their return trip from the Pacific, to scout what we now call the Grand Tetons and Yellowstone. His tales sparked the beginning of the influx of explorers and homesteaders to the West.

Much more recently, Devil's Tower became the focus of the movie, Close Encounters of the Third Kind, about more technologically advanced 'explorers' arriving, not in covered wagons, but in spinning UFOs.

Geologists say that this huge knuckle of rock in front of us was created with a flow of molten magma 60 million years ago, pushing its way up into a layer of sedimentary rock. It cooled and shrank and separated into flutes or columns. The exposed volcanic mass eroded through centuries of wind, rain and snow into today's knob of a monolith. We're looking at the core of an ancient volcano, made of a rock called phonolite that is iron-rich red and glistening in the bright sunlight.

In contrast, the Sioux creation story tells of seven girls being attacked by a giant bear. They crowd onto a small rock and pray to the stone gods to save them. The gods cause the rock to grow higher and higher until the girls are out of reach. The bear continues to claw for the girls, though, causing the striations in the rock. The girls meanwhile, escape to the sky to become the sisters in the constellation of Pleiades.

Though no bear is chasing Nathan and Kenny, they quickly scramble up and over the rocks. They exude energy and joy and I catch it too as I climb the path. Nathan is partway up the rocky base ahead of Kenny, and I collect some snow from below the rocks. I expertly make a snowball—some childhood skills are not lost—and throw it to Kenny, higher up the slope. He catches it and throws it on the top his head gleefully. He makes his own snowball and tosses it to me and another one that he throws high into the air. Then he runs up the trail to catch up with Nathan who is continuing to clamber over the rocks.

"Hey, look at the climbers!" Nathan calls down to me and he points up to the cliff.

Sure enough, there are several tiny figures on the nearly vertical walls. They are testing their skills, with ropes and pulleys, helmeted and climbing along the vertical channels to reach the top. They belay each other—securing themselves at the end of a rope—with rappel devices, descenders and harnesses attached to the sturdy belts around their waists. More than a thousand brave souls a year climb almost 900 feet from the rocky base to the flat summit of sagebrush and grass. They each look like a fly on the wall.

"They're calling to each other," Nathan calls again, "in climbing lingo."

And then I too notice the distant calls.

The climbers, Nathan and Kenny, make it up the rocky slope to the bottom of the wall. Looks are deceiving. It is so much further than it looks. What must climbing the wall be like?! When the boys decide to turn around, I do too, from halfway up the path.

"You guys got a good workout and I did too. It felt great," I say. "And the day couldn't be more beautiful."

"Yes, yes," they answer, as we all approach the van and hop in. "That was cool, nice, interesting, pleasant and scary," Nathan says. "It's time to go to Montana."

Montana is just a short hop across the border on Highway 112, and then it will be a short stay for us.

"This will be my 35th state," Nathan says with pleasure. "Being in as many states as possible is my biggest reason for making this trip."

"It will be my 17th state," Kenny calculates.

"Montana has strong similarities to Wyoming, and you've probably realized it too," I say to the boys. "They share the Rocky Mountains, shaped by glaciers, in the west. They both have plains in the east, outside our windows, the domain of the Plains Indians centuries ago. Mining for minerals and gems is a big industry in both states. And cattle grazing and skiing and touring. Put us in that last category. As for skiing, I haven't skied in these western states but I've skied in Switzerland. Does that count?"

"Not really. Montana is on top of the U.S." Nathan says. "It borders three provinces of Canada—British Columbia, Alberta and Saskatchewan. I remember that from before I started kindergarten. Montana is a wide state and geographically is the fourth biggest state in the United States. Tomorrow we'll be east of here in Canada's province of Manitoba."

"Hey, guys, if we could do an Evil Knievel jump west to Idaho, we could cover more territory. He jumped the Snake River Canyon in Idaho in a rocket-powered skycycle. Montana claims him as a resident for all of his growing-up years. There's another fantasy idea for you, Kenny!"

"I have a car, but I'd like to get a motorcycle in the future instead of a car," Kenny admits. "I like to drive fast. I'd like to do daredevil tricks. Doing things on my own that are almost dangerous is fun. Pushing myself to the limits of what I'm capable of."

X

August 2014

X stands alone.

Well, OK, X does have a lot in common with all the other 25 letters of the alphabet. From A through Z, each letter is called a *single letter word*, is defined as a letter and is given grammatical status as a noun. But, let's take just the letters A, I and O and we can see that they, unlike the rest of the alphabet, are used freely by themselves in conversation and writing. A, distinguished as the first letter in our English alphabet, is called, by any standard English dictionary, an indefinite article. The letter I is called a pronoun and is a chemical symbol for iodine. O gets the label of an interjection and is a chemical symbol for oxygen. The rest of the alphabet letters have to have another letter or more attached to the one letter, as in the expression OK, for it to gain more spots in the grammatical categories and to make it a word (except as a letter word or a chemical symbol). Just as Scrabble demands that we use more than one letter for all the words that we make on the Scrabble board.

The exception to this formulation is the unique, versatile X. This letter X is the most recently added letter (800 BC) to what was to become the modern English alphabet and the Ancient Greeks were the ones who added it. All 25 other letters originated in Egyptian hieroglyphics, moved on to the Phoenicians and then to the Ancient

Greeks where X was added. What became our entire 26 letter English alphabet went then from the Greek to the Etruscans and on to Ancient Rome and then to old English and at last to modern English.

To display X's versatility, in addition to being labeled a noun, X is called a verb as in X-ing. X is also a consonant. X is an abbreviation, as in *Christ* through the ages of different languages and then arriving as X in English to make Xmas. X is also an adjective as in an X-rated movie.

X is filled with symbolism and is itself a symbol, unique and set apart from A to Z, all of which add to its mystery. It crosses all lines from the legend of the prehistoric Pagan cross of a shepherd's crook crossed with the grain flail of Assur or God of resurrection and humankind, ancient religions such as apostate Judaism where the X symbol is for change, Freemasonry using X as the sign of the Egyptian sun God named Osiris, the occult using X as a symbol for transformation, to the X's found in medieval and renaissance art and then appearing on up through modern culture and in popularized usage.

The number of words beginning with X or having X used in the word is impressive for its infrequency. Words beginning with X in our dictionaries add up to the last in the frequency of being seen of all the 26 letters that are used to begin a word. There are from 100 to over 400 words in dictionaries (I counted 361 in one listing) of words starting with X. And for the use of X within a word, by one calculation, X is seen in a word from 0 to 15% of the time in frequency. X is the 3rd least frequent letter to be used in a word, with Q and Z being seen the least. I've looked at lists of words using X in the word and they add up to thousands, but still less than all the other letters except Q and Z. Words beginning with just A alone that have X in them have added up to 256, by one listing that I counted. And there are 24 other letters that start words (beside X and A) with X in them that I didn't count so it must add up to at least a couple of thousand. But X still makes its appearance in words much less often than any other letter outside of Q and Z. So we value the few words that do use X, especially in the game of Scrabble because they count.

Scrabble players, like my grandson, memorize spellings of thousands of words. The point count of X is 8 (q and z have 10 points each) so X has high value to use in a word. Almost any player (even me) knows the five 2-letter words with x: xu, xi, ax, ex and ox. And we should know the 36 3-letter words: xis, zax, pyx, kex, vex, vox, box, cox, fax, fix, fox and 25 more to add up to 36, in order to have an edge on our opponent. Counting all 5, 4, 3, 2 and 1-letter words with X in a Scrabble dictionary probably adds up to hundreds, which varies with each new edition of the Standard Scrabble Dictionary.

X's relative rarity and its other unique features attract our attention and add to its appeal. When we see it we notice it like I do when I see several pages filled with a variety of X designs displaying an imaginative and historic beauty.

History, from ancient times on, has given X a mystique with its symbolism in the paintings on walls of Egyptian temples and pyramids and on mummies of Egyptian pharaohs discovered with arms crossed in an X across the chest. Why? Coats of arms and flags of many countries and religious drawings through the ages show X prominently in their designs. Academics have made a stab at explanation and observers like me can speculate as well. Crossing arms in an X in old and new cultures of Japan is said to mean no good. X stands for a crossing of blood lines, as on a coat of arms. X means blockage. Stop. Don't go any further with sexual advances or attempt to hit or assault with a weapon. Crossing your arms is an attempt to protect one's self. It also means, like an oath or genuflection, I swear I am telling the truth, as in 'cross my heart and hope to die.' Some see X as symbolizing sexual union. The modern culture has made the Playtex Cross Your Heart Wire-free bra. A film comedy from 1946, called *Cross Your Heart* with Betty Hutton, led to another Cross Your Heart song in the movie, game series and DVD enterprise (as only our modern culture would create off of old ideas): Castlevania: The Dracula X Chronicles. And back to Egypt, the X is the sign of Osiris, the great sun God. The letter X reigns.

A lot has happened with X over centuries of time that make it a standout, a knockout and a magnet for free-form use in our modern age. With irony, I've said that X in the dictionary takes up almost the smallest space for a letter category of words. Call it virtually invisible. But in the more visible worlds of commerce, technology, science, medicine, math, cyberspace and the fiction and fantasy of movies, X has sprung to life with imagination and creativity that catches your attention and it has holding power. How can you forget X-generation or Gen X?

This one letter X has captured the imagination of movers and shakers throughout the world of communication and contributes to and is at home in the mentality of catchy, brief and 'get one's attention in a second of your time and the blink of an eye' that prevails in our culture.

Here is some of what we've had and what we have. X-Files, The X Factor, Xena:Warrior Princess, X-Men and X-Play have all appeared on the TV screen. At least a dozen movies have been entitled just X. More movies, with titles like X2, X3 (etc), Xa, Xala, Xenia, Xingu, XOXO and XY, have come and gone with new ones likely to come.

Expressions fill our talk and writing almost automatically, like clichés. X marks the spot on a map for treasure or in a parking lot.. XXX is for love at the end of a letter or email. "I exed her out of my life" over the meanness your friend showed to you. If I tell you that I have the X on you, I have put you in a less-advantaged position with whatever secret information I have about you. Gestures like cross your fingers mean 'I hope and wish.'

X-Products gun accessories, Germ X sanitizers, Gas-X flatulence reducers and a host of other companies and products with an X meet up with you in the world of commerce. Brand X is the research product that is keeping you in the dark. With X as an abbreviation for extra, clothing lines are sized with XS, XL and XXL.

Technology brought us the Microsoft Games Console called Xbox, and then Apple put out the Macintosh operating system called OS X at the turn of the decade in 1999. Astronomers record Planet X as the name of a hypothetical planet. And Project X is a secret in many areas of life.

Voters mark an X on a ballet for their choice of candidate or proposition in an election. We put an X on forms to show us where to sign. X out the things you have done on your to-do list or agenda and the things you don't want to do. I put a big X on top of my handwriting to show the parts that I want to delete.

Science has made up words with X. The X-chromosome paired with the Y- chromosome determines the male sex. Two X's make for a female. The abnormality of XXY is called Klinefelter's syndrome.

Mathematics and science, both using math to solve the big questions (witness Einstein's formulas to explain Relativity and other workings of the universe) are filled with XXX's. The most used X is probably the multiplication symbol in arithmetic. In 1637, Rene Descartes started using X in math equations and we continue today using X in algebraic equations and in formulas and in language where X represents the unknown. X is the name for an independent variable or unknown value. In Roman numerals, X denotes the known number 10.

The field of medicine is loaded with X words. The letter X by itself has 32 definitions in a dictionary of medical abbreviations. The definitions include cross-section, removal, transverse and roentgen (as in x-ray). Those 4 definitions leave 28 more medical definitions (as in the X used in mathematics) for the reader. Dorland's Medical Dictionary, © 2012, has 145 words beginning with X, including such hefty ones as xanthomonadaceae (family of organisms) and xenocytophilic (affinity for cells derived from a different species). Across the spectrum of our use of words, X itself seems to be of a little different species with its unique traits, usage and image.

And then there are all the playful rhyming words ending with X. They pop up in poetry, children's books and fun chatter. We have tux and flux, pox and lox, tax and wax and sax and lax, nix and mix and six and fix, just pick a vowel. Dr. Seuss, in *One Fish, Two Fish, Red Fish, Blue Fish*, gives us "In yellow sox I box my Gox. I box in yellow Gox box socks." And with the e-vowel we have flex and hex, ex and rex, specs (no x) and vex, and most prominently and commonly—sex.

A few other common X words for us not to neglect include xanthan (gum), xaxis (axis in a plane in math), xe (pronounced as Z and is the chemical element symbol for xenon), xenophobe (one who is fearful of what is foreign), the proverbial, old news as the X-word in children's dictionaries, xylophone, and the exotic place of Xanadu (yes, there are some proper nouns in the dictionary listings). Xanadu suggests a place that the letter X might reside. Both hold a mystique. Young and resilient they are, strange and alien and smacking of the forbidden, all of which fit both Xanadu and X. The letter X takes up a small space but what a place. I think X will be holed up in our fascination for a long time.

As you exit this essay, soon to be ex, I sign off with an extra X in the female sex, yours truly XX.

YEARS

2005

I just celebrated seventy years of life on this earth. About thirty assorted relatives, friends, and college students came at my invitation and with food to share, on a sunny, warm, Sunday afternoon in November, to my rented house in Wisconsin. All of us communing the joy of a great life, with many more years to come.

Now, I wasn't sure that I wanted to announce to the world my age. Seventy years is a lot of years. People usually think that I am in my 50's and I say, "Thank you very much. I feel like a teenager." If I choose to say my age in years, they are surprised that I am as old as I am. As the years have passed by, I have become reluctant to answer anyone's query about my age.

I have my reasons. For one thing, society has prejudices about 'older' people and I don't want to be set apart from others because of my years. Don't relegate me to the fringes. I do not wish to be out of the mainstream. I look young, feel youthful, have the fun of a kid, and I act like a babe, seeing every event in my daily life—from doing stretches, when I wake up in the morning, to watching the sun make shadows of trees on the grass—as an amazing adventure. Add a bounding curiosity with the world around me and inside me and a fascination with the self, essence, heart, soul, and substance that make up my life. I am an active participant in this game called living.

A contrived category of assumptions and expectations does not suit me, nor, I think, does it suit the rest of society. "She is 80 and alone, she won't find romance." "He is slow in moving around the house, he is showing his age." "They don't get around much anymore." "Be careful." "Get your rest." "Watch your step." Conditions and admonitions, that can be demeaning, seem to come with added years.

But in a way, I realize that I am indulging myself. All of my concerns with what society thinks and does with age strike me now as a little cosmetic, perhaps not as important as I have made it. I live my life and whatever others think or do about my age or theirs or others' numbered years are their concern, not necessarily mine.

With a little soul searching, I admit another reason for my avoiding saying my age in years. I do not want to die. Death was always a distant abstraction in my unconsciousness. People close to me didn't seem to be dying, until I was well grown up. Death did exist for me, however, in the Bible. As a young regular Sunday School attendant, I knew the verses.

"For the wages of sin is death." "Yea, though I walk through the valley of the shadow of death." "O, death, where is thy sting?" I made a connection between fear, comfort, and courage, and death. But the concept of life ending still seemed remote.

In my more secular, adult years, my reading took me to Willa Cather's *Death Comes for the Archbishop*, a moving account of a good life coming to an end, and John J. Gunther's *Death Be Not Proud*, a courageous effort to try to save a son's life. When I was in college, my eight-year old niece died. Years later, my parents died, then my four brothers, one by one, over a decade. And then my husband's life came to an end. Death was real and I was shocked and I grieved. My own death, though, still seemed a long ways off.

But I am seventy now. Those years give me pause. Though I intend to live a lot more years and I take good care of myself and I am wearing well, the reality of death is stronger. And my accepting the certainty of eventually leaving this earthly realm and being ok with it is getting a little easier. I resist it less. I love my life even more. I do not have the comfort of an absolute belief in my soul living on, but it may be so, and I hope for and can imagine the beauty of my core being joining up with other spirits on another plane. I feel the delight of the reunion.

Seventy years young! My party celebrants know and now, I am telling the world! It is good to be seventy! Cheers all around! I resist no more. Whatever my allotted time on our planet is, I am happy to be here. And in the mysteries of life, at some unknown moment in endless time, my time will move away from an earthly form. And I can say "A life well lived. The riches abounded. The treasures and pleasures were plenty. The trip has been glorious. I have navigated well the bumps and lumps on the road. I am ready to move on."

Ethel Erickson Radmer

ZEST

November 2014

Xenophon of Athens, in ancient Greece, was born in 431 BC and lived for 77 years until his death in 354 BC. He was a pupil of the philosopher Socrates and an author of at least 14 books. In "The Symposium" Xenophon wrote, "We (Xenophon and Cleinias—a possible mute character present in his mind's eye) are the true inspirers who infuse some subtle fire into amorous souls and thereby raise them to new heights of being . . . we give them a zest for toil that mocks at danger . . ." (I love H. G. Dakyns' choice of words in his translation). So, the concept of zest and a fire within was part of their thinking—approximately 2400 years ago!

The Greek word *schistos* or *skhistos* means 'cleft' (referring to lemon cut to give relish or zest to a drink) and was probably the first word we know that transmuted through the centuries to the English word zest. By the 18th Century in England zest referred to a quality that adds enjoyment to something—like a lemon's tang and snap add flavor to food.

So, you can see in the etiology that the word and meaning of zest has an evolutionary history, possibly derived from ancient times. According to a 19th Century (1895) writer SALMOND (Fordyce), acknowledged in capital letters in the Oxford English Dictionary © 1991, "The Greek people had an almost unrivalled zest for life."

By that it seems appropriate to trace this powerful word's history to Ancient Greece.

I have found dozens of more modern-day, alike words and meanings. All are related to our inner core being of aliveness. The word piquancy overlaps two meanings of zest—an agreeable flavor and a hearty enjoyment. Zest is living life with a sense of excitement and adventure. It is exuding energy, performing wholeheartedly, vivacious, living well, enjoying things to a high degree and being a force of nature.

Zest is showing boundless curiosity about all the details in life (that's me!). Mindfulness, as in the Buddhist's being fully present in every moment of their day. Zestfully smell the freshly mown grass. Appreciate the colors in the sunset. Zest is animated spirit and brimming enthusiasm in everything we pursue.

Love your life more. Let your zest manifest from glowing outside and inside with joy on up to shouting and cheering from the rooftops. Zest means exuberance, radiating, spiritedness, verve, esprit, elan, buoyance, jauntiness, carefree, animated, gusto, levity, good time, sprightliness, rompishness, frolicsome, lustiness, mirthful and sparkle. And using all forms of the word we will have zest and its plural zests. Be zestful. Have a zesty time. Own zestfulness. Enjoy others zestfully. Try not to be zestless. Notice your zested pleasures.

If you need to or if your enthusiasm is waning aim at renewing your zest for life. Get a jump start with nutritional considerations, meeting sleep needs to restore and heal all parts, accomplishing physical feats, keeping your mind and brain alive with quiet to calm and stimuli to enliven. Put yourself out there, take chances, expand your thinking enough to see the humor in all our lives. And then rev life up a notch. Accelerate the fun and satisfaction. Expand to a high energy level that radiates. Zest can be front and center for every one of us.

It's great to have that fire in your belly to get as much as you can out of life within and without. And, speaking for myself, I think zest has coursed through my vessels since I can remember. Curiosity is big. I want to know more about almost everything. Music and art have filled my life with passion. It comes from within. What others achieve and enjoy is an inspiration that adds to my inner drive to get the most out of my day.

We hear and read about people with special challenges and hardships and how they surmount them with high energy, sheer will and a zest for living. Rebecca Alexander, author of *Not Fade Away*, is one of those amazing people who stand out with their accomplishments and verve. She started going blind and deaf when she was a teenager, due to a genetic condition called Usher syndrome. With that diagnosis, she was driven even more to do what she wanted to do including being an athlete competing in extreme endurance races, earning degrees to be a psychotherapist and living alone in New York City and getting around by herself. You know what it takes to do that? Zest! A zest for life. She has it in spades. She uses the word herself. "People often tell me that I am an inspiration, for my zest and enthusiasm for life, my lack of self-pity, my acceptance of what I'm facing . . . " While living, Rebecca says she is storing up images and sounds to draw on later as the senses shut down. That takes zest to even think to tuck away clear pictures of what you see and sounds of the voice and retrieve them for pleasure at a future time!

There's something about challenges to one's living that make zest stand out and make one determined to live life to the hilt. That is why we notice other's zest. Their expanded living is against a backdrop of limitations that might damp down one's attitude toward life. But people have risen above any limits and appreciate every day. And remember that we *all* have challenges. I dare say that no one is immune!

Anita Moorjani had a near-death experience that she wrote about in *Dying to be Me*. With terminal cancer, she was at death's door, left her body to an expanded experience of love and light and then she returned. No trace of the cancer was found and she was a changed person. "I just felt blessed to be alive and to get a second opportunity to express myself here. I no longer wanted to waste even one minute of the great adventure. I wanted to be as much *me* as I could possibly be and savor and taste every delicious minute of being alive! . . . If everything I do each day is driven by passion and a zest for living, then I'm 'being'." And she's not alone. Many near-death experiencers come back with a renewed zest for life. And I will add, if you have zest it grows on itself—a self-perpetuating urge for life's experiences.

Michael J. Fox, who has Parkinson's disease, has a zest for life that has no bounds. He does not feel damaged or frail or any embarrassment so he is not blocked emotionally in doing all the things that he does. He doesn't let negative emotions, especially fear, get in the way of his zestful life. And that includes playing golf, ice skating and starring in a TV series. His style is full-fledged, no holds barred and full-throttle. Humor, appreciation for the good and joy fill his being. Zest has free rein.

There are many others (and perhaps you) whom we might know in our own circles or hear and read about who have challenges in life and elevate their intentions to get the most out of life that they can. When they might feel life slipping away they rise up and zestfully have a go at living in surprising ways. A benefit for the rest of us is that we are inspired to also have a zest-filled life.

And here's the ultimate teacher for all of us of a zestful life, for Anita, for Roger Ebert (did movie reviews while having consuming cancer and was described as being famous for zest for what he loved -- and hated) and for the World Trade Center workers making phone calls home to say "I love you," as the towers melted to the ground. This great teacher is death. When we face the possibility of death at any moment in our lives we can choose to let an enthusiasm for life permeate our being. Why do you think so many people who find they have a terminal illness change their lives and appreciate every moment of every day? They have confronted death and know that they want to get the most out of life possible in a lifetime that could end at any moment. A zest for life is front and center in their consciousness.

Forays into the food culture bring zest, zesty and zestfulness into books, famous chefs and TV shows and into companies and products. With the new year coming and in spite of my paying no attention to the TV chefs or to people's resolutions through the decades I will embark this one time on making a New Year's resolution or call it a recipe of my own for us and for the coming year and to be continued for a lifetime. But this recipe will also serve as the signoff for the end of this essay and the *finis* or *fait accompli* for my book of essays.

NEW YEAR'S RECIPE FOR HUMANITY

Start out with one earthly finite life. Select ingredients thoughtfully. Acknowledge behavior, emotions and thinking that exist but leave a bad taste in your mouth and a heavy weight on your heart and mind. Notice, measure and try on for size the feel good traits. Nice, kind, loving, happy, giving, thoughtful, fun, generous, helpful. Talents are expressed, skills manifested, abilities channeled into useful, pleasurable, humorous and serious exploration and educational endeavors and accomplishments. Knowledge gained is shared to learn. Mix them together and add the one spice that trumps them all, that makes life all good and worthwhile. ZEST. With zest you can bake just right in the heat of whatever surrounds you—conflict, grief, cheerfulness or adventure. Your zest for life will nourish you and sustain you. It will carry you through all the lumpy places in life to the inner core being of aliveness. A lifetime, however short or long, will taste better, digest well, look beautiful, smell glorious, sound tempting and feel sensational. It will satisfy all the senses. May you have a zest for living every day of your life. Life is a gift and zest empowers us to make the most of it!

e e radmer November 22, 2014